Alaska's
Inside Passage
With Terry Breen

Cruiser Friendly Guide to

Alaska's
Inside Passage
With Terry Breen

Illustrations by
Mary Sterner
Lawson

Cruiser Friendly Publications
Albuquerque, NM 87104
w w w . c r u i s e r f r i e n d l y . c o m

Breen, Terry
    Cruiser Friendly Guide to Alaska's Inside Passage with Terry Breen

1. Travel – Alaska
2. Travel – Cruise – Alaska

First published 2005, 2007 and 2010 by Terry Breen

ISBN-13: 978-0-9787661-8-4

Printed in China
by Gold Printing Co., Ltd.
www.goldprinting.cc

The Cruiser Friendly Onboard Guide to Alaska's Inside Passage has been written as an accurate and reliable source of information with respect to the subject matter. It is a travel guide and reference, and not meant as an authoritative text, or for navigational purposes. No monies were exchanged for the endorsement of any business or service. Third edition updated 2010.

Cruiser Friendly Publications
Albuquerque, New Mexico
www.cruiserfriendly.com

Designer: David Edwards, Albuquerque, NM
Cover photo: Sergiu Ghita
Drawings and edits: Mary Sterner Lawson
Maps: Terry Breen and David Edwards

TABLE OF CONTENTS

It was in early 2003 sailing the Straits of Magellan. Terry Breen was on the bridge when she conceived the idea to write this book.

This is a new approach and an original presentation of The Last Frontier. It is a privilege and a great pleasure for me to write these words on the first page.

Captain Jean-Marie Guillou

PREFACE

At long last, you've made it. You're in Alaska -- The Last Frontier.

Alaska is still wild and untamed. Its lure is intoxicating. In Alaska nature has the power to transform even the most city-hardened hearts. You'll never be the same. Man is dwarfed by the proportion of nature. Everything is bigger and better: trees grow taller, mountains loom larger, eagles soar higher, and summer days linger longer. The bounty of the land is surpassed only by the abundance of the sea where otters play in kelp-filled coves, salmon return for their heroic upstream migration and humpback whales gently teach their young to feed in the clean, cold, oxygenated water. Embrace Alaska and awaken your soul.

I love Alaska. The few months I am privileged to spend here each summer nourish and sustain me for the rest of the year. I have been blessed to have cruised all over the world; however, when asked which cruise experience I love most, my answer is Alaska. During your week onboard you will be transported to more destinations in Alaska than could be visited by land in an entire month. You will see nature like you've never imagined. Summer in Alaska means eagles, wildflowers, glaciers, whales and fresh-baked pie. Alaska is waiting.

May you too be blessed by the spirit of Alaska.

Have a wonder-filled cruise.

Terry Breen

Storyteller

INTRODUCTION

The name Alaska comes from the Aleut word, "Alyeska," or Great Land, and great indeed it is. Alaska is the land of the biggest and the best. First of all, Alaska is BIG. If Alaska were a country it would be the 17th largest in the world. If you divide Alaska in half, Texas is still the third largest state in the United States of America. When Alaska became the 49th state on January 3, 1959, it was so big it was originally divided into four time zones; in 1983, those four time zones were consolidated into two - Alaskan and Aleutian/Hawaiian. Despite the enormous size of the state it still has only one telephone area code – 907.

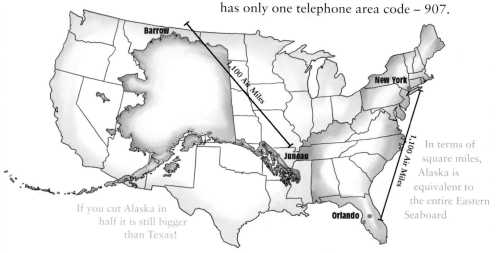

If you cut Alaska in half it is still bigger than Texas!

In terms of square miles, Alaska is equivalent to the entire Eastern Seaboard

Size and Distance Comparison

Alaska is 571,951 square miles in area, and, according to the 2009 census, has a population of 692,314 -- that's approximately 1.1 persons per square mile. Alaska has the youngest population outside the state of Utah with 27% of the population under the age of 18. The average Alaskan is a 32-year-old male, and men still outnumber women about 2 to 1.

ALASKA'S TALLEST PEAKS

Mt. McKinley	20,320 ft.	Mt. Sanford	16,237 ft.
Mt. St. Elias	18,010 ft.	Mt. Vancouver	15,700 ft.
Mt. Foraker	17,400 ft.	Mt. Churchill	15,638 ft.
Mt. Bona	16,421 ft.	Mt. Fairweather	15,299 ft.
Mt. Blackburn	16,390 ft.	Mt. Hubbard	14,950 ft.

ALASKA HAS:

- Over 110,000 glaciers.
- 42,000 miles of coastline.
- The tallest peak in North America: Mt. McKinley 20,320 feet.
- The world's tallest coastal mountain range, the Wrangell-St. Elias Mountains.
- 17 of 20 tallest peaks in North America.
- 3,000 rivers.
- Over 3 million lakes of 20 square acres or more.
- World's longest protected waterway – the 1,000 mile long Inside Passage.
- 16 Lighthouses.

Aleutian Islands

Bering Sea

Dutch Harbor

Alaska has 50% of all the glaciers in the world, covering about 29,000 square miles; scientists estimate that only 10% have been named or studied. Along with Scandinavia and Chile, Alaska is one of the few places left in the world where tidewater glaciers still exist.

Alaska's Inside Passage is 1,000 miles long and 200 miles wide, stretching from Ketchikan to Skagway and the Pacific to the Canadian border. There are 55,000 people spread out over 1,000 islands, over half living in the state's capital of Juneau.

Chukchi Sea

ARCTIC OCEAN

Barrow

Nome

Fairbanks

Anchorage

GULF OF ALASKA

Juneau

Kodiak Island

INSIDE PASSAGE

PACIFIC OCEAN

Ketchikan

Alaska is the most northern, eastern and western state in the United States. Obviously it is the most northern with one third of the state above the Arctic Circle; but it is also the most western and eastern state because the Aleutian Islands extend out so far they cross the international dateline into the eastern hemisphere at 165 ° E!

FACTS

ALASKA IS
"THE GREAT LAND"

PART 1

1 ALASKA IS "THE GREAT LAND" FOR ITS BEAUTY

Nowhere else is nature more dramatic than in Alaska and there is no better way to see and experience its coastal beauty than from the deck of a ship. Sail through glacially carved fjords to ice-filled bays or watch eagles soar over tree-covered islands; around every turn a magic moment awaits. Alaska is so exciting it is hard to pull yourself away from the awe-inspiring scenery. No wonder it is one of the most popular destinations in the world for cruising.

Alaska is divided into six geographic regions: Southeast maritime, Southwest maritime, Bering maritime, Aleutian Islands, Arctic and the Interior. The "Inside Passage," where most cruise itineraries concentrate, lies within the Southeast maritime region, also known as the "panhandle" of the state.

ARCTIC

One third of the state of Alaska lies north of the Arctic Circle above 66° 33' N. This is the land of summer's Midnight Sun and winter's glorious displays of the aurora borealis. Contrary to popular opinion, the Arctic is not the frozen wasteland of story books. Long summer days expose rocky beaches and mossy meadows studded with wildflowers. With the dark days of winter, sea water freezes; snow and ice cover the land. However, recent increase in temperature is causing Arctic ice to melt rapidly, causing a loss of habitat that endangers many animals, including the polar bear.

INTERIOR

The largest region of the state, the interior or "the bush," is the most dramatic for its miles of uninterrupted, rolling tundra altered by extreme, seasonal temperatures. From October to March, cold arctic winds wail down from the north, causing temperatures to fall to -85° F. In contrast, mid-summer temperatures soar in excess of 100° F. Much of the interior contains continuous permafrost, perpetually frozen ground that does not melt regardless of the season. Just as in the Arctic, climate change is affecting the interior where regions of permafrost are melting, causing habitat change and increased emission of methane gas. Though most of the interior is virtually uninhabited, Fairbanks, population 75,000, located on the Tanana River, lies within the interior and is the second largest city in the state.

BERING MARITIME

Exposed to the bitter cold of the Bering Sea, the western frontier of Alaska is an open windswept corridor. Extreme temperatures and driving rain, sleet and snow shut down this portion of the state for a portion of the year. Only the hardiest of souls live in this region, eking out a living from commercial fishing and subsistence hunting.

FACTS

Bush Families?

The region known as "the bush" of Alaska occupies over 50% of the state. Originally meaning any place inaccessible by road, the bush is still home to a small but hardy group of people who choose to live a frontier lifestyle. These "bush families" live in remote areas where their closest neighbor may be 200 miles away. Surviving off the land, their only contact with the outside world may be a short-wave radio and the occasional visit by a bush pilot who brings the mail, medicine and home study materials for families with school age children.

ALEUTIAN ISLANDS

Extending out into the Pacific, the Aleutian Islands are the westernmost reach of North America. Part of the Ring of Fire, the Aleutians were created by volcanic activity and uplifting. Make no mistake; this area is still volcanically active. The most recent explosive eruption occurred in March 2009 on Umnak Island when the Okmok Volcano erupted. Over 600 rocky islands make up the Aleutians which were named after its indigenous inhabitants, the Aleuts. From Attu, farthest island west within the archipelago, Asia is only 221 miles away.

SOUTHWEST MARITIME

Taking in the area around the Kenai Peninsula, the Southwest maritime region is home to most of Alaska's population. Unlike the Southeast maritime region, where winter temperatures are mild and rain falls year round, the Southwest maritime, located at 60° N, has colder winters and drier summers. The drier climate attracts more residents. The largest city in the

Volcanoes, earthquakes and tsunamis

As one of the most active areas along the Pacific Ring of Fire, Alaska is prone to earthquakes as well as volcanic eruptions. Earthquakes take place all the time; however, the one that Alaskans will never forget hit on Good Friday, March 27, 1964. Outside of Anchorage the strongest recorded earthquake in North American history rocked the entire North Pacific coast. The earthquake was a magnitude 9.2 and caused a huge tsunami that engulfed many coastal communities. The final death toll was 131 people; 119 died in the tsunami.

FACTS

state, Anchorage, population 279,243 (2008), is located on Cook Inlet, which is in the Southwest region. Also along Cook Inlet is Mt. Redoubt, a towering strato-volcano that recently blew its top in a 15,000 foot eruption in May 2009.

Located in the northwestern corner of Prince William Sound is the magnificent College Fjord. It is said that it contains the greatest concentration of tidewater glaciers in one fjord anywhere in the world - there are 20. The area was first charted and explored by 30 geologists taking part in the 1899 Harriman Expedition; they named the glaciers after their alma maters. The tradition continued until 1911, when the Muir Glacier was named after the naturalist John Muir.

SOUTHEAST MARITIME

A majestic ridge of high uplifted coastal mountains and hundreds of islands make up this picturesque region. Together they define the sheltered waterway known as the "Inside Passage." Moist, on-shore air warmed by the Japanese current creates heavy clouds that stall at the base of the Coast Mountains. Huge amounts of rain fall at lower elevations. Within the Southeast maritime region is the city of Ketchikan. Famous for its liquid sunshine, it is called the "Rain Capital of North America," as it averages 162 inches a year. As clouds rise above 6,000 feet moisture falls as snow which contributes to the ice that feeds the many glaciers of the state. Mist and clouds shroud the islands and hills most of the year, producing areas of dense temperate rainforest. The 17 million acre Tongass National Forest is the largest in the United States. Temperatures along the Southeast coast are moderate. The majority of Alaska's communities are located in "Southeast." The state's tourism industry is focused here as an increasing number of cruise ships and excursion boats discover the beauty of cruising coastal Alaska.

ALASKA IS "THE GREAT LAND"
FOR ITS FORESTS AND FLOWERS

Visitors to Southeast Alaska love how green it is. Long, warm summers and cool, rainy winters keep the coast lush and verdant. The soil is rich and loamy. With rainfall in excess of 150 inches a year, Southeast Alaska contains dense temperate rainforest. The vast Tongass National Forest protects western hemlock, red and yellow cedar, cypress, maple, black cottonwood, yew, pine, and, the state tree - the Sitka spruce. Vegetation ranges from shaded ferns and marshy muskeg, to open meadows of tall grasses and wildflowers. Late spring and early summer you will see fields of blossoms including lupine, wild iris and the state flower, the Forget-Me-Not. This delicate plant has a pleasant, sweet fragrance used to scent many local products.

PLANTS COMMON TO SOUTHEAST ALASKA

Pacific red elder	Harebell	Black lily
Cow parsnip	Yarrow	Blue bell
Skunk cabbage	Leafy aster	Salmonberry
Fiddlehead fern	Canadian goldenrod	Devil's club
Fireweed	Stream violet	Blueberry
Deer cabbage	Pearly everlasting	Chocolate lily

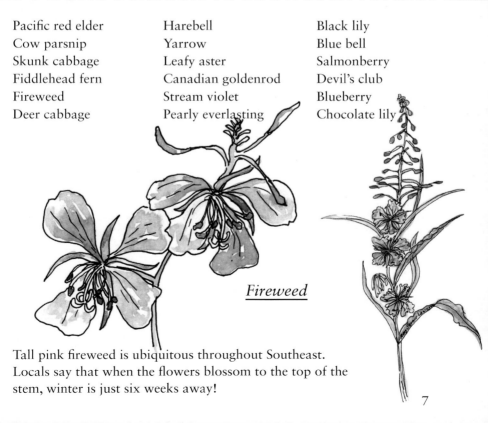

Fireweed

Tall pink fireweed is ubiquitous throughout Southeast. Locals say that when the flowers blossom to the top of the stem, winter is just six weeks away!

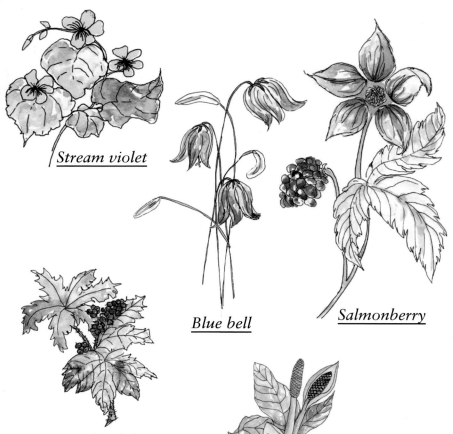

Stream violet

Blue bell

Salmonberry

Devil's club

For centuries the Tlingit have used the prickly Devil's club for many medicinal uses.

Skunk cabbage

Blueberry

Black, Chocolate, or Skunk lily

TREES COMMON TO SOUTHEAST ALASKA

Alder
Lodge pole pine
Willow

Black cottonwood
Mountain ash
Western hemlock

Spruce Tree
Cedar
Sitka Spruce

Western hemlock (Close Up)

Sitka spruce

Spruce tree

Cedar (yellow and red)

9

3 ALASKA IS "THE GREAT LAND" FOR ITS WILDLIFE!

Southeast Alaska abounds with wildlife. The land, sea and sky are filled with creatures big and small from fur to feathers. It is a thrill and a privilege to experience nature so closely.

Though hundreds of species inhabit all parts of the state, during your cruise you may be lucky enough to see one of Alaska's "Big Five" – whale, bear, moose, sea lion and mountain goat.

MARINE MAMMALS OF SOUTHEAST ALASKA

Many of the marine mammals that make Southeast Alaska their home reside here all year. Sea otters, fur seals, harbor seals and Steller sea lions feed upon fish and crustaceans. Some, however, like the humpback whale, are seasonal residents coming for the long days of summer when krill and phyto-plankton are plentiful.

Whales, porpoise and dolphin belong to the order known as cetaceans. As mammals, all cetaceans breathe air and bear live young. They travel in groups called "pods." Alaska is home to eight different species of whales (minke, right whale, pygmy right whale, Beluga whale, sperm whale, gray whale, narwhal and humpback) and four species of porpoise (killer whale, Dall's porpoise, harbor porpoise and Pacific porpoise.)

ALASKA WILDLIFE CHECKLIST TO KEEP TRACK OF EVERYTHING YOU SEE. GOOD LUCK!

_____	Black bear	_____	Dall's porpoise
_____	Brown bear	_____	Killer whale
_____	Moose	_____	Humpback whale
_____	Mountain goat	_____	Bald eagle
_____	Dall sheep	_____	Marbled murrelet
_____	Fox	_____	Harlequin duck
_____	Sea otter	_____	Loon
_____	Steller sea lion	_____	Puffin
_____	Harbor seal	_____	Pigeon guillemot

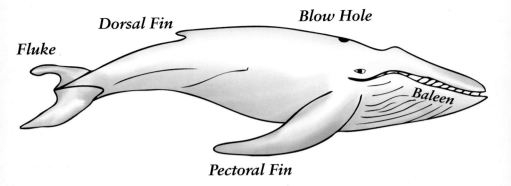

Dorsal Fin

Blow Hole

Fluke

Baleen

Pectoral Fin

Cetaceans are divided into two sub-species, toothed and baleen. As the name implies, toothed whales have teeth, are carnivorous and usually beaked in appearance. Baleen whales have a mesh-like filter in their mouths used to strain krill, plankton and small fish from sea water. This brush-like filter is made of keratinaceous protein similar to human fingernails.

Humpback whales

The most popular baleen whale in Alaska is the humpback. Humpback whales are migratory. One of the great mysteries of nature is the humpbacks' 3,000 mile annual migration. True to their course, a recent study noted that tagged whales never deviated more than 10° off magnetic north!

How long do humpbacks live?

For many years, marine biologists believed humpback whales live between 35 – 55 years; as a result of recent discoveries that statement has now changed. Noticing that plugs of wax incrementally build up in the whale's ear, marine biologists are using these plugs to date the animals in the same way tree rings are used to date trees. Now they estimate that humpbacks live up to 80 years.

FACTS

How do you spot whales?

The easiest thing to see is the "blow" or exhalation of vapor from the lungs. Humpback whales have lungs about the size of a Volkswagen van, and when they come to the surface to exhale the air rushes out at over 300 mph. This blast of warm, moist air produces a burst of vapor, which looks like spray. Whales usually come to the surface to breathe every 4 – 9 minutes. When they surface the back and the dorsal fin is exposed. Baleen whales like humpbacks, grays, and minkes have two blow holes which produce a low, heart-shaped blow. The small triangular dorsal fin is located midway down the back. When they dive, the back curves forcing the fluke up. Seeing a beautiful fluke slicing through the water is poetry in motion. However if you see that fluke going up it means the whale is diving down and could be gone for as long as 45 minutes! Toothed whales have just one blow hole. When a killer whale surfaces, its blow shoots up like a geyser. The next thing you see is that tall, black, rudder-like dorsal rising up. Killer whales do not normally show their flukes when they dive.

During the winter they stay in the warm waters surrounding coastal Mexico and Hawaii where they mate and give birth. During this time they do not eat. Humpback calves are born with no body fat and could not survive in the cold water of the north. Staying close to mom the calf will gain up to 200 pounds a day during the first days of life. In the spring, once the calves are strong enough, the pod travels north to the cold waters of Alaska where they do nothing but feed all summer. At 40 feet in length, 40 tons in weight, adults need to feed a lot. In one scoop a humpback whale can take in 750 gallons of sea water, straining out 100 pounds of fish per gulp! On average, an individual humpback consumes 2,000 - 3,000 pounds of food per day. Marine biologists identify humpbacks by the shape and color of their unique flukes or tail-fins. The name humpback comes from the graceful curve of the whale's spin. The Latin name, *Megaptera novaeangliae*, means Great Winged New Englander; a name given by the early whalers because the humpbacks have the longest pectoral fins of any whale. At 15 feet, these incredibly long fins resemble graceful, underwater wings!

Humpbacks often engage in cooperative feeding. Several whales will exhale a net of fine bubbles around a school of small fish and then, on cue, will simultaneously come up underneath the prey, scooping it up in their gaping mouths. In lunge feeding, whales extend the accordion like folds of the throat and gulp their way through concentrated areas of food.

During your cruise you may see humpbacks exhibiting the following behavior:

Pectoral fin slapping
The whale raises its long pectoral fin and slaps it on the water, sometimes propelling itself around from side to side.

Fluke slapping or tail lobbing
The whale submerges the forward portion of the body exposing the fluke, pounding it against the surface of the water; marine biologists interpret this to be a defensive act or a way to define territory.

Sky hopping
The whale pulls its torso out of the water enabling it to better see its surroundings.

Breaching
The whale jumps entirely out of the water, slapping its body down, producing a huge splash. Many people expect to see whales breaching all the

How big are humpback calves?

As a mammal, a humpback female gives birth to one live calf after a gestation period of 11 months. The calf measures 15 feet in length and weighs 2,000 pounds. Curling its tongue to form a tube that fits into the female's mammary folds, the calf slurps up milk that is so high in fat (up to 50%) it is comparable to drinking the richest ice cream. The calf gains roughly 7 pounds everyday for the first year, during which time it is never separated from its mother.

time. This is not the case. Seeing a whale breach is about as likely as seeing a falling star. Breaching is a rare thing; however, once started, a whale may continue for 30 – 40 minutes. Marine biologists are not entirely sure why whales breach: some say it is defensive behavior; others are convinced it knocks off bothersome barnacles, and then there are those who say maybe it's just fun!

Orcas

"Killer whales" or orcas are the most common toothed whale in Alaska. They feed primarily on salmon and seals. Killer whales are actually the largest species of dolphin. They grow to 30 feet in length, are black (or dark grey) and white in color, and have a tall, black, dorsal fin with a white saddle-patch located behind the dorsal fin. Dorsal fins on males can be over 6 feet high. The size and shape of the dorsal fin is unique. Like the markings on the fluke of a humpback whale, dorsal fins are used for individual identification on killer whales. Called, "sea wolves," killer whales hunt in pods. They use sonar to echo-locate their food, bouncing sound waves off prey to chase and corral it.

When do we see whales?

Whale watching takes patience. Your naturalist knows where pods have been feeding and will announce when you approach those areas. Humpbacks are often seen in Snow Passage, Lynn Canal, Sitka Sound, Auke Bay and Point Adolfos. The best spots for killer whales are around Robson Bight and Blackney Pass in British Columbia. They stay close to shore during salmon runs, which happen in late summer and early fall.

Marine biologists group killer whales by resident and transient pods. Resident pods stay in one area year round feeding primarily on fish; transient pods migrate and usually feed on smaller marine mammals. Occasionally, an individual, usually a male that does not fit into the pod, separates away. They are known as rogues.

Killer whales have behavioral patterns similar to humpbacks. However, they also cavort and play. After feeding they jump, spin, and flip out of the water, sometimes tossing their young high into the air. Many "tricks" performed in artificial environments are actual behaviors seen in the wild.

Porpoise

Dall's porpoise and harbor porpoise are often sighted from the ship. Playful, they seem to enjoy swimming in front of the ship's bow and behind in the wake. As the name suggests harbor porpoise concentrate in harbors and bays. Dall's porpoise are often seen in open water and reach about 3 – 4 feet in length with black and white markings similar to that of a killer whale which is why the two are often mistaken. It's easy to know the difference; in addition to the disparity in size (the killer whale being much larger) the Dall's porpoise also lacks the tall dorsal fin. Dall's porpoise congregate in large pods sometimes numbering in the hundreds and are known to be the fastest marine mammal.

Seals and Sea lions

The furry side of Southeast Alaska's marine mammal population includes seals and Steller sea lions. Throughout your cruise keep an eye out for a seal or sea lion, as they may poke their heads up next to the ship at any time. Smaller and shyer, harbor seals are best spotted during the early spring when females haul-out onto small growlers, using them as safe havens for the birth of their young. At this time of the year, females and pups are plentiful in places like Johns Hopkins Inlet in Glacier Bay, Tracy Arm, Yakutat Bay, and College Fjord. Up on the ice, once dry they appear blonde in color with brown spots. At a distance they look like black crescents or caraway seeds – you will have to grab your binoculars to get a good look. Extremely territorial, Steller sea lions return to the same rookery year after year. Weighing up to 2 tons, bull males dominate an extended family known as a "harem." One harem can have twenty females. More gregarious than seals, sea lions cavort together, often pulling themselves up out of the water to have a look around.

Harbor Seal

Was that a seal or a sea lion?

Seals and sea lions look similar to the untrained eye. But here are a few tips to tell them apart. Sea lions have articulated flippers that bend like elbows, enabling them to climb. Seals do not. When you see a bunch of critters snoozing out on a buoy or pier they are probably sea lions. Sea lions are larger than seals and they can haul the top quarter of their bodies out of the water. In contrast, seals rarely expose more than their snouts. Finally, in case you are looking closely, sea lions have exposed ear folds - seals do not. Now you know a trade secret.

TERRY'S TIPS

Otters

Called nature's clowns, otters love to play and frolic and are genuinely fun to watch. Alaskan sea otters grow to be about 4 – 5 feet in length. They live in social groups known as rafts. Otters swim on their backs, paddling forward using their back feet. They feed on clams, shellfish, and fish and will use small stones as tools to crack open shells. Using their stomachs as tables they carefully pick through the juicy bits of clam or crab they have collected then spin in the water to clean off their mess. As they swim they produce a very distinctive "V" shaped wake. Females carry their young on their chests. Otters are fastidiously clean, constantly rolling themselves in the water to flush away debris. When not feeding they are usually grooming their coats. Their luxuriant pelts were prized by the Russians who traded them with the Chinese. So valuable were sea otter pelts they were referred to as soft gold. The exquisite nature and warmth of sea otter fur comes from the fact otters have no body fat. Unlike other Alaskan marine mammals --- whales, seals, sea lions, and walrus --- otters do not have blubber or protective body fat to keep them warm. Instead nature has given them a multi-layered coat that traps pockets of air close to the body providing insulation. To stay warm otters must keep their coats clean and fluffy to trap much-needed air. That is the real reason for the constant grooming and spinning. Otters sleep in the water and often wrap themselves and other family members in long strands of bulb kelp. The tubular kelp not only helps to keep them joined but also acts as additional insulation as well as breakfast when they awake.

During the 1989 Exxon Valdez oil spill in Prince William Sound, the sea otter population was severely affected. Once heavy crude oil covered their bodies, oil soaked otters could not keep themselves warm and died from hypothermia. Today the sea otter population of Prince William Sound is once again thriving.

LAND MAMMALS OF SOUTHEAST ALASKA

Wild animal habitat exists throughout Southeast Alaska whether you are sailing past a broad beach, hiking a forest trail, flying over glacier covered peaks, or walking out your front door. Humans in Southeast Alaska are accustomed to unannounced visits by four-footed friends, like the time when passengers at the Ketchikan airport were surprised to see a black bear cub taking a ride on the luggage carousel.

One of the sayings about wildlife is that it's called *wild-life* for a reason. This is still wilderness - not a zoo; in other words, there are no guarantees. Admittedly, there are times of the year that are better than others to see certain animals. However, unlike the sea that remains more constant, fluctuation in temperature, rain, as well as an increased human presence, can affect and disturb animals on land. Every effort will be made onboard your ship to insure that you will have the optimal viewing opportunities both on land and sea without negatively affecting the local wildlife.

Brown bear

Here's what I hope you will see and a few tips on how to spot them.

Bears

Everyone wants to see a bear. In Southeast Alaska there are two different types of bear -- brown bear and black bear. Black bear are the smaller of the two, measuring 4 – 7 feet and weighing 125 – 500 pounds. The largest black bear found to date (North Carolina) weighed 880 pounds. Black bears are primarily herbivores, eating roots, berries and vegetation, but they won't say no to a fat salmon if offered. Brown bears are omnivores; they eat anything and everything. Brown bears are much larger than black bears, averaging 7 feet in height and 700 pounds. The largest brown bear found (Canada) weighed 1,400 pounds! The brown bears on Kodiak Island in Southcentral Alaska, on average, are the largest in the world. Traditionally, brown bears that live in the interior are known as "grizzlies," while those that live along the coast are "brownies." Of the two, brownies grow larger than grizzlies based upon the greater availability of food. Many people argue that grizzlies with their silvery fur and pronounced shoulder hump are different, and give them the separate genus name *ursus arctos horribilis*. However, biologists account for the difference in the bears' coloring as a by-product of a thicker fur needed in the colder climate of the interior and a larger shoulder hump as a response to more digging. Bears are not only strong but fast. They can run 30 – 40 mph. And finally, bears are prodigious swimmers reaching distances of up to 9 miles offshore. Both brown and black bears average two cubs born in the spring. Bears are most easily seen in the late summer along salmon spawning streams.

Cuddly teddy bear toys have brought bears into the homes and hearts of

When do we see bears?

Alaska is known for its bears. Many people expect to see polar bears on their cruise. Though polar bears exist in Alaska they do not live in the southeastern portion of the state. On your cruise look for black and brown bears.

If you are cruising to Southeast Alaska in the spring, bears are just starting to become active after their winter hibernation. A good place to find them is along rivers, streams and beaches foraging for easy food. Spring is also the time when you might be lucky enough to see a female with cubs, usually two.

In the late summer, bears congregate along the salmon spawning streams where activity is intense as they aggressively bulk up for winter. Check with your tour desk for excursions to bear-watching platforms which have been built to offer tourists a chance to safely see the bears. The State of Alaska Division of Wildlife Conservation offers information on wildlife viewing. www.wildlife.alaska.gov

TERRY'S TIPS

millions of people. However, the real thing is far from its plush cousin. Bears are wild. Bears can run. Bears can climb. Bears can swim. Bears can maim and kill. Before venturing off on a wilderness trail familiarize yourself with the safety recommendations of the U. S. Park Service. Free pamphlets and booklets are available throughout Southeast Alaska. Avoid surprising bears in any environment. During the summer months bears are known to wander into the outskirts of town. If you come upon a bear and it does not see you, move away quickly and quietly. If the bear has seen you, keep your distance; speak in a normal voice and gesture with your arms to identify yourself as a human not another bear. Bears will often stand on their hind legs to better see you; this is not an indication of aggression. Move away from the scene and notify authorities. Be bear-aware!

Mountain goats and sheep

Cruising through the fjords of Southeast Alaska gives you an excellent opportunity to look for mountain goats and Dall sheep. Mountain goats usually travel in small family groups: the male (billy), the female (nanny) and the kids. Their shaggy fur absorbs light, giving a yellow appearance to the coat which helps to distinguish goats from patches of snow. Their hooves have a special suction-cup like adaptation that allows them to scale sheer cliffs better than Spiderman. If you see a trail of cream-colored dots walking up the side of a steep mountain, get out your binoculars --- it's probably goats.

Dall sheep

Because they are more elusive, you are less likely to see Dall sheep from the ship. With their impressive, curled horns, they prefer the solitude of higher ground and mountain tops. If you take a flight over the mountains this is the time to look for Dall sheep.

Moose

Moose are the largest terrestrial animal of Southeast Alaska. With their knobby knees, shaggy beard and huge antlers they can reach 8 – 10 feet in height. Moose are members of the deer family. As big herbivores their favorite habitat is marshy grasslands. Though the television series Northern Exposure was not filmed in Alaska, the depiction of a moose walking through the small town is quite real. Every once in a while a moose will saunter through!

TERRY'S TIPS

Watch for sheep, goats, and moose

A great place to see Dall sheep and mountain goats is on the highway outside of Anchorage between Girdwood and Potter. If you are traveling to or from Anchorage keep an eye out on the land side of the roadway; the goats and sheep like to perch on the rocky cliffs opposite Turnagain Arm.

The very best place to spot a moose during your cruise will again be on the highway or train between Anchorage and either Seward or Whittier, depending on which port your ship uses; keep an eye out near Moose Pass and Portage Glacier.

On your way to or from Ketchikan, you may spot some of the elk that were recently introduced onto Zarembo Island near Snow Pass.

Sitka black tailed deer

The most common deer of Southeast Alaska, the Sitka black tailed deer, can be found everywhere. Don't be surprised to see them on the beaches of small islands. Deer can swim.

Wolves

Many of the epic tales of Alaska include stories about wolves. Gray wolves are endemic to Southeast Alaska and still can be found in remote areas. Coyotes and red fox also live in this part of the state.

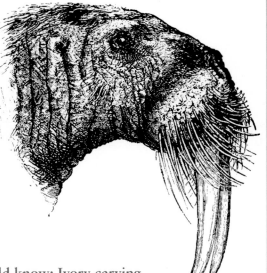

To buy or not to buy; that is the question.

Throughout the gift stores and galleries of Southeast Alaska you will see for sale items made of animal hides, bone, and ivory. Is it legal to purchase these things and are you adversely affecting the animal population? Here are a few things you should know: Ivory carving is done by the Native people of the Arctic and Bering Sea regions. Only Native Americans are allowed to have and use raw ivory. Fossilized ivory from walrus as well as prehistoric mammoths and mastodons is legal. Native people still live on subsistence hunting and are allowed to take ivory-bearing game. In addition to food, the skins, bones, and tusks are used for clothing and crafts. According to the State Department of Economic Development, Native hunting has minimal impact on overall animal populations; for example, walrus populations are greater than they were 100 years ago. Proceeds from carving form a substantial part of Native income.

Important: If you are planning on bringing ivory into Canada, to avoid fees, obtain a permit available for free from the gift shop where your ivory is purchased.

Baleen, bone, pelts, mounted skin, trophy heads, and wood products are legal to purchase.

Ulu and scrimshaw knives must be placed in your checked luggage. Ship security may require you to surrender these knives until disembarkation.

TERRY'S TIPS

BIRDS

Avid birders will have a hard time keeping up with the numbers of birds in the skies of Southeast Alaska. A partial list of the most common birds includes:

Sea Birds:

Gulls (5 species)
Shearwater
Oyster catcher
Petrel
Cormorant
Arctic tern
Heron
Plover
Sandpiper
Murre
Murrelet
Loon
Grebe
Duck (mallard, harlequin, merganser, scoter)

Land Birds:

Bald eagle
Raven
Ptarmigan
Stellar's jay
Blue grouse
Rufus hummingbird
Hawk
Kestrel
Crane
Dove
Owl

Crow
Magpie
Chickadee
Wren
Robin
Thrush (3 species)
Waxwing
Starling
Warbler (4 species)
Sparrow (5 species)

Pigeon guillemot

Marbled murrelet

27

Raven

Willow ptarmigan

Puffin

Arctic tern

28

Eagles

One of the most thrilling sights to see is a bald eagle in flight. Once on the verge of extinction, the bald eagle was taken off the endangered species list on July 4, 1994. Along with the raven, the bald eagle figures prominently in the culture of the Native Americans of Southeast Alaska. The two family lineages or moieties of the Tlingit people are said to be descended from either eagle or raven ancestors.

Fun facts about bald eagles:

- Eagles mate for life. The mating couple returns each year to the same nest, which can grow to weigh two tons.

- In the wild, eagles live an average of 30 years.

- Juvenile bald eagles are entirely brown. They appear larger than their adult parents because they have elongated training feathers. These feathers that they will lose upon maturity help the young eagle learn to fly and soar.

How to spot a bald eagle

The mature bald eagle is fairly easy to spot. With its white hood and white tail feathers it stands out against the green trees. Eagles prefer the upper branches of the tallest trees. Scan the tree line and if you see something high up that looks like a golf ball, use your binoculars to focus in on the bird. Sitka harbor is a great place for eagles, as is Ketchikan. In Tlingit, Ketchikan means, "Eagle Wing River." As you enter or leave Ketchikan look at the dead tree on the south side of the small island in Tongass Narrows at channel marker "7" – there is an active eagle's nest with a pair that returns every summer.

Bald eagle

- At about four to five years of age the juvenile loses its brown feathers and takes on the distinctive white hood and white tail feathers. This is also an indication that the bird is sexually mature and ready to take a mate.
- Both male and female eagles have the same colored plumage.
- Eagles prefer to scavenge rather than hunt and can be seen feasting along the beaches especially during salmon spawning season.
- Eagle talons once engaged are hard to retract. When eagles spy a fish in the water they must be very certain they can lift it up. If the fish is too large, the weight of the fish will bring down the eagle and it will drown.
- Eagles have hollow bones that allow them to support wings that can span six feet!
- It is illegal to possess eagle feathers unless you are a Native American.
- The bald eagle became the symbol of the United States of America in 1782 in spite of Benjamin Franklin's reference to it as, "a bird of bad moral character."

Only in Alaska...

Everyone loves hummingbirds and that is especially true for the people of Southeast Alaska. Every summer they put out feeders for the little birds. But they are also very diligent about removing them at the end of the season. The presence of a feeder late in the summer is certain doom for the unfortunate bird that has not yet started its migration south. A few years ago a "cheechako" (newcomer) living in Juneau kept her feeder out longer than she should; the result was one wayward bird that was in town too long. As soon as neighbors heard they contacted local experts who caught the little bird. Now faced with getting the bird back on its natural track arrangements were made to put the bird on an Alaskan Airlines flight to California where it was set free! Well, that's what I was told...

FACTS

FISH

The cold, clean water of the north Pacific coast combined with millions of lakes, rivers and streams makes Alaska the ideal habitat for hundreds of varieties of fish. It's no wonder that commercial and sport fishermen consider the waters of Alaska to be some of the best and most abundant in the world. In Southeast Alaska you will find trout and Dolly Varden. Along the coast you can dig for clams as well as collect edible urchins, barnacles, and mussels. At deeper depths you'll find abalone and crab including tanner, Dungeness and the world famous Alaskan King crab. The open sea is home to shrimp, octopus, Arctic grayling, herring, and of course, halibut and salmon. Halibut are bottom fish growing to gigantic size. In 1996 in Dutch Harbor, the world record 459 pound halibut was caught. However, most avid fishermen with limited time (like those aboard cruise ships) prefer to try their luck with salmon.

Salmon

There are five different species of Pacific salmon known by two different names; king or Chinook, silver or coho, sockeye or red, pink or humpies, and chum or dog. Salmon are the only fish that live in both fresh and salt water. The life cycle of the salmon is probably the most fascinating of any fish. Salmon lay their eggs in freshwater streams. As the eggs hatch the fry stay in those same streams until they reach the stage when nature tells them they are mature enough to head out to deep water. For the rest of

A real fish story

King or Chinook salmon is the largest of the five species. Alaska holds the official world record for the largest salmon caught, a 97 pound 4 ounce Chinook, in the Kenai River in 1995. Now that's a BIG salmon!

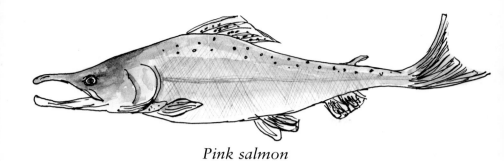

Pink salmon

their lives they will live in the salt water of the open sea. Depending on the species, salmon live at sea for 2 – 5 years. Proponents of "wild salmon" say that spending their lives moving freely through the clean, cold open water makes the salmon stronger and healthier, and therefore more tasty and nutritious. At maturity, something goes off in that little salmon brain that indicates it is time to return home. Traveling sometimes thousands of miles, salmon will miraculously return to the very stream in which they were spawned. Salmon pack on fat that will be burned upstream, as once entering freshwater they do not feed. To maximize their reproductive advantage their bodies take on new shapes and characteristics; fangs grow, gnarly humps form. Once this metamorphosis starts salmon are no longer prized for consumption. It is now left to nature to see who will survive the trip. Those that were strong enough and lucky enough to make it will lay their eggs and die, completing the life cycle. Within a few weeks, fry will be hatched and the cycle begins anew.

Wildlife watching frustration?

Invariably, you will hear people with binoculars glued to their faces say in exasperation, "I don't see anything." Relax. In Alaska the world is disproportionately LARGE. For example, mountain goats appear to be nothing more than tiny cream colored specks on a hillside. Now, consider the distance of the ship from the shore, the elevation of the hill and the size of the goat. Look closely at the scrubby moss on the side of the hill. Use your binoculars and you'll see it's not moss after all but full growth trees probably 90 feet tall. Now figure if that tree is 90 feet tall, how big is that hill? Hmmmm.... the hill is more like a mountain. No wonder that goat looks like a tiny speck; Alaska's landscape is unimaginably big.

TERRY'S TIPS

4 ALASKA IS "THE GREAT LAND" FOR ITS GLACIERS

Without a doubt one of the most spectacular sights to see during your cruise will be a glacier. There are over 110,000 glaciers in Alaska, which is 50% of all glaciers in the world. A highlight of most cruise itineraries is a day of scenic sailing through areas of active glaciation. It is exciting to know that up in the mountains those patches of white that appear to be snow and ice, upon closer inspection are indeed glaciers. Some are bigger than others; some are dirty, some are clean; some cover high mountain valleys, others reach the sea. So what is a glacier?

A glacier is a "river of ice." Glaciers and rivers have many characteristics in common; they are both in constant motion; they both meander and carve out the landscape creating valleys; and they both carry along rock, rumble and debris, depositing it along its path.

Evidence of ancient glaciation exists throughout Southeast Alaska. Thousands of years ago a huge, heavy 4,000 feet deep sheet of ice covered most of the land. The weight of the ice smoothed down and rounded over hills at lower elevations. Those peaks that were tall enough to be free of the glacial ice remained sharp and jagged. As the ice slowly melted back and retreated, where it had once covered the land, graceful "U" shaped valleys now appeared. The ancient glaciers are gone, but new glaciers continue to flow down beds carved out during ancient times.

What is a "fjord"?

A "fjord" is a glacially carved valley that has been filled in by the sea. Characteristics of a fjord are a steep shoreline, mountains that plunge straight down into the sea, very deep water, and, at the entrance or mouth, an undersea wall or bar of moraine left by the glacier. Fjords occur in Scandinavia, Chile, and New Zealand. In Alaska, many waterways were named by mariners who did not know how the body of water was created. Though it may be named Lynn Canal or Tracy Arm, technically all these places are still fjords.

FACTS

How old is the ice?

Cruise brochures and travel guides often refer to glaciers as "millions of years old ice." Though the glacial beds in which the glaciers are flowing were carved out during the last Ice Age, the ice you see today is not that old. Due to the large amount of snow that falls in areas around coastal Alaska, ice builds up quickly, feeding the glacial systems. In areas of heavy snowfall, the ice viewed at the terminus of a short, fast moving glacier may be only 75 years old! In larger glaciers like Hubbard, the ice at the terminus may be as old as 1,000 years, which is old -- but not that old in geological terms.

A glacier forms when snow falls, builds-up, and does not melt off. In Southeast Alaska, precipitation falls as snow above 6,000 feet. Because of the combination of the altitude of the tall coastal mountains and their latitude - being located so far to the north – snow falls all year at higher elevations, making conditions perfect for creating glaciers in Alaska.

Let's imagine that somewhere along the Coast Mountains there is a high mountain bowl located above 6,000 feet. Snow will fall and accumulate all year. As the bowl fills the snow will turn to ice. Ice continues to build up as more snow falls. The weight of the ice compresses the lower layers, changing the lacey ice crystal into a more compressed pellet-like form of ice called firn. As more snow falls more firn forms. Hundreds of feet of this heavy firn weighing down upon itself eventually squeezes out all the air in between these compressed crystals and turns the ice into glacial ice.

As the glacial ice continues to build up, soon it will overflow its area of containment. Instead of shattering off the edge as regular ice would, the malleable glacial ice molds itself like frozen fudge slowly finding the path of least resistance. The ice starts to flow downhill, gravitating towards the lowest elevations. The glacier acts like a huge conveyor belt; the new ice created at the top or "source" pushes the old ice forward down the mountain, filling the nearest valley. The source can be one single mountain bowl or a huge plain called an icefield. Icefields feed several glaciers. A glacier can be 100 miles long or it can be 1 mile long. A glacier is a glacier as long as the crystalline structure of the ice has changed regardless of size.

The glacier is always moving downhill with gravity. However, you may have heard glaciers referred to as advancing and retreating. That sounds as

How to tell if a glacier is advancing or retreating

Unless you are glaciologist or a local resident who watches glaciers closely, it is hard to tell. But again, there are tricks. If a glacier is growing, it will be full and thick, pushing new ice down the mountainside, encroaching into existing trees and vegetation. However, if it is retreating, the shrinking terminus and thinning sides of the glacier will expose bare rock which was previously covered by the once larger glacier.

though some glaciers move backwards. Not the case. The terms are used by glaciologists to refer to the net gain or loss of ice on a glacier over the course of a year -- is it growing or shrinking? An advancing glacier has a net gain; a retreating glacier has a net loss. If a glacier gains 900 feet in ice, but loses 700 feet at its terminus through melt or calving, it still grew 200 feet. However if that same glacier would have melted 1,000 feet it would have a net loss of 100 feet and would be shrinking or retreating.

As you travel around you will hear your ship's naturalist and guides refer to various parts of the glacier. The source or head of the glacier, as previously discussed, is the area from which the glacier grows. It could be a small bowl at the top of the mountain or a huge icefield miles away. The top of the glacier is called the surface; it is the largest portion of the glacier in area. The end of the glacier is the terminus. The base is the bottom, where the ice meets the frozen ground beneath.

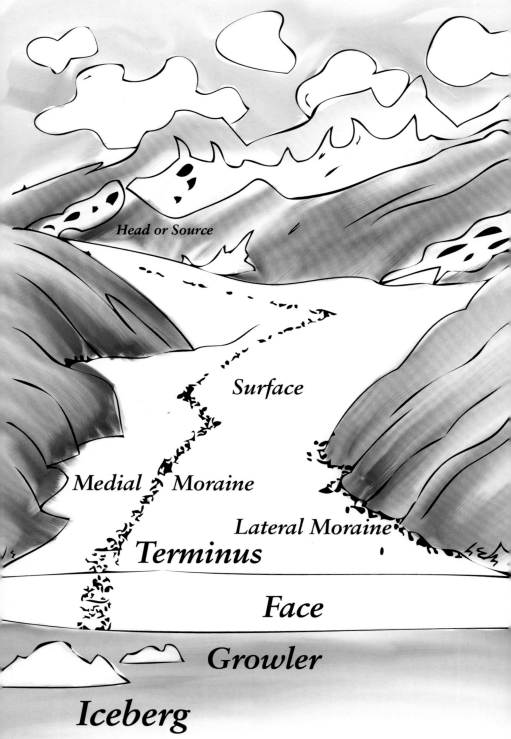

Head or Source

Surface

Medial Moraine

Lateral Moraine

Terminus

Face

Growler

Iceberg

Icequakes?

You don't have to be a geologist to know that glaciers creak and crack, boom and rumble as they make their way down the mountain. With all that weight and force you'd imagine that the shifting and sudden movement would create energy. Well, it does. Each shudder and shake creates an icequake. They are substantial enough that seismologists can track and measure them. In Antarctica magnitude 7 icequakes have been measured. Recently researchers studying Bering Glacier reported up to one event every thirty seconds! More icequakes occur during periods of warming and melt that accelerate the glacier's movement. Climatologists are monitoring icequakes as an indicator of climate change.

Geologists give glaciers different names depending on where they are geographically located. Continental glaciers cover huge regions with massive sheets of thick ice. Greenland and Antarctica are covered by continental glaciers. These are so large ice pushes out laterally in all directions like pancake batter over a griddle. When the ice exceeds the support of the land it often pushes out into the sea forming an ice shelf. When ice breaks from an ice shelf it produces huge icebergs. These bergs which sometimes can be as big as small islands are the kind of icebergs that pose problems for ocean-going vessels. It was an iceberg from Greenland that sank the

How do you tell if you are looking at a glacier?

From a distance it is hard to tell the difference between ice or snow and a glacier. Consider the characteristics of a glacier, knowing it is bending and stretching down the mountain: the pliable nature of the ice causes surface tension to form. That tension is relieved by cracks or crevasses. These cracks appear and disappear as the glacier moves downhill. Since regular ice does not do that, the presence of crevasses is an indication you are looking at glacial ice. When these crevasses appear, they expose that deep glacial blue color, your second clue that this is a glacier.

Why is glacial ice blue?

I recently had a great chat with an optical physicist who explained to me in great detail why glacial ice is blue. Here's the condensed version; because of the unique nature of the ice, all the colors of the spectrum are absorbed by the ice except blue. The long wavelengths of the color red are absorbed by the ice so they disappear. The shorter blue wavelengths are scattered and bounce around longer making the ice appear blue. The more compressed the ice, the deeper the hue of blue. When the outer layer of glacial ice is exposed to the sun or wind, it begins to melt and refreeze. Each time this happens it incorporates more air back into the ice: more air lightens the hue of blue. Ice that appears white or clear has incorporated so much air that the crystals are back to that of regular ice or snow which scatters the light quickly.

FACTS

Titanic. Glaciers that creep down a mountainside but have not made their way all the way to the bottom are called hanging glaciers. When a glacier does make it to the valley floor and ends on dry land it is called a valley glacier. If that valley glacier pushes out into the flatland of the valley floor it is called a piedmont glacier. And finally, if the glacier ends in the sea, it is called a tidewater glacier.

Once the ice calves off the terminus and drops into the sea it becomes an iceberg. By definition, to be an iceberg there must be at least 10 feet of ice above the surface of the water. If you remember your junior high school science classes, icebergs only expose 10% of their surface, so a small berg will have 90 feet below. Anything smaller than that is called a growler, or in Alaska you'll hear it called a "bergie bit." As the ice shatters or melts into smaller pieces, that is called brash ice. In the spring you will often see harbor seals and their newborn pups hauled out on the growlers. With the increasing number of cruise ships to these areas marine biologists have been observing how the seals are being impacted

The face of a tidewater glacier represents about 1/3 of the entire depth of the glacier; the remainder is underwater. Remember, the glacier is not flat and is not floating on the surface of the water but rather fills the entire valley. The part that continues underwater is called the tongue. Ice can

Glacier Watching

Tidewater glaciers are the most popular type of glacier to see from a cruise ships because - the best view is from the sea! You will only find them in Chile, Scandinavia and Alaska. The highlight of a visit to a tidewater glacier is seeing it calve. So, what does that mean, exactly? Notice that the "terminus" of the tidewater glacier - or the end of the glacier where it meets the sea - looks like it has been sliced off forming a wall. This wall is called the face. It is being pushed forward by the formation of new ice at the glacier's head or source. Calving happens when the ice is expelled from the face into the sea. Technically this is called ablation. There are no particular times when glaciers calve. As with most things in nature you just wait and watch. As the glacier moves it makes a groaning noise; this is your clue that something is happening. Try and keep an eye out around the area where you heard the sound. Sometimes the ice will crack, sounding like a sharp gunshot or a huge boom. Native Americans would call this white thunder, as it sounded like thunder emanating from the ice. Showers of ice may appear. This is a good sign. If your timing is right you will see huge pieces of ice break off and crash into the water, producing an enormous splash and a rolling boom! Watch the waves. Sometimes after a big chunk of ice has calved off, it will cause a piece of the tongue to break off creating a shooter!

break off unexpectedly from the tongue and shoot up, making it very dangerous for ships and boats that get too close.

In glaciated areas you will notice the water looks chalky and opaque. As glaciers move downhill they grind stone into a talc fine powder called silt. The silt is carried along by the melt water off the glacier. That melt water is fresh water, and as it accumulates it produces rivers and streams that drain into the sea where the lighter fresh water containing the silt stays suspended on the surface of the heavier salt water, producing a film of chalky or muddy discoloration. Visitors may think the steely gray water running through some Alaskan streams is polluted, but now you know to fear not – it is only glacial silt.

Some glaciers appear dirtier than others; some look very clean and white, while others are covered with what looks like dirt and debris. Like a river, glaciers grind up and carry along material in its path that is called moraine. Moraine is not dirt but rather crushed rock and rubble. It is sterile and takes a long time to collect enough organic material to create soil and support vegetation. When the moraine builds up and deposits along the glacier's flanks it is called a lateral moraine. When it covers the terminus it is a terminal moraine. And when two glaciers meet uphill, squeezing together two lateral moraines it forms a medial moraine, just like the medial line when two lanes of a freeway merge.

You can tell how many glaciers have merged uphill by counting the number of medial moraines at the terminus.

All glaciers are moving downhill at different rates. The speed at which they move depends on snow, temperature, climate, and incline. Most glaciers are inching along; some are moving at a few feet a day. In 1986, and again in 2002, for a few days Hubbard Glacier in Yakutat Bay started to move at unprecedented speed of 140 feet a day. It was traveling so quickly it went from a surging glacier to a galloping glacier. Hubbard is one of the few glaciers in Alaska that is still advancing. It is 6 miles wide, about 1200

Does anything live in a glacier?

Many birds and mammals live near the glacier but only one thing lives in it – ice worms. It is not a joke. The ice worm is about one inch long and resembles black spaghetti. They live just below the surface at temperatures slightly above freezing. They feed on algae that grow on the surface of the ice as well as pollen that gets blown in. They come to the surface to feed making sure they don't stay out too long lest they get picked off by a hungry bird. In February, the town of Cordova celebrates an Ice-worm Festival.

FACTS

feet deep, and 76 miles long. It is the largest tidewater glacier in North America. In 1986, when Hubbard surged it dammed off nearby Russell Fjord, producing a glacially created lake. Water levels rose at a perilous rate as melt water accumulated, diluting the sea water and threatening the population of salt water fish. The community of Yakutat feared it too would be flooded if the old Situk riverbed was reconstituted. Fortunately the ice dam broke, the fjord drained and the waters levels equalized. However a similar event happened again in 2002, leading glaciologists to believe it is just a matter of time before Hubbard closes off the fjord, permanently creating Russell Lake. As of summer 2010, Hubbard appears once again to be on the move. The face of the glacier is about 400 feet from closing off Russell Fjord; heavy ice conditions have prevented ships from getting up Disenchantment Bay. Just as changes in Columbia Glacier warranted its closure to the public in the 1990s, we may soon see restrictions on Yakutat Bay as well. Just another reminder that when all is said and done, Mother Nature is still in control!

FACTS

Glacial ice is special. It is not like regular ice in your freezer. It has unique properties. Because it has been formed under such extreme pressure glacial ice:

- Has different crystalline structure than regular ice.
- Takes longer to melt than regular ice.
- Is plastic (unlike regular ice that shatters and breaks, glacial ice can bend and stretch).
- Appears blue.

Historically people have come to Alaska from every place, for every reason. Alaska has always been seen as a land of opportunity from the first Native Americans who came in search of big game to the prospectors looking for gold and later oil. Alaska's population has waxed and waned with the boom and bust of its economy. Today's population of 692,314 residents still represents less than 1.1 people per square mile. With most residents concentrated in the city of Anchorage and the towns of South-east, it's mind-boggling to realize that the rest of the state remains virtually uninhabited.

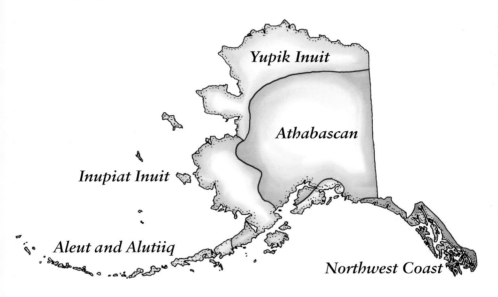

THE NATIVE AMERICANS

Native people are an integral part of the history and culture of Alaska from prehistoric times to the present. Roughly twenty per cent of the state's population is Native American, belonging to one of five major cultural groups: the Athabascan tribes of the interior; the Yupiq, Cu'piq and Inupiaq (Eskimo) Inuit of the Arctic; the Aleut & Alutiiq of the far west, including the Aleutian Islands; and the Tlingit of the Northwest Coast people of Southeast Alaska. Facilitated by the advent of the white

trappers and traders, the name "Eskimo" was ascribed to the people of the far north. The term meant, "Those that eat raw meat." It was not a nice description. In 1977, the Circumpolar Conference of Native People decided that they would be called by the name they call themselves which is "Inuit." Slowly that change is taking place throughout Alaska and Canada.

Archaeological evidence tells us that early man entered into North America in waves beginning about 12,000 – 14,000 B.C. During that time 20% of the earth's water surface was frozen up at the poles, exposing 20% more coast line. The shallow strait that now separates North America from Asia was dry, allowing man to walk across. As the exposed shoreline was also broader than it is today, man filtered down the coast as well as through the interior, settling where conditions permitted. The last wave of migration came about 6,000 B.C. when the Inuit arrived by sea from Asia.

Each of the four Native American cultural groups has its own unique adaptation to the environment. Learning to survive in extreme conditions, the ice house known as an igloo was built by the Inuit as temporary shelter during a hunt; the sea-going Aleut created swift skin-covered boats built to withstand savage waves; and the Athabascans sewed furs into air-trapping garments that kept them warm when winter temperatures plummeted. It was the Northwest Coast people of Southeast Alaska that were blessed with milder temperatures and bountiful resources that developed one of the richest and most sophisticated cultures in the Americas.

Northwest Coast Culture

This is both a geographic description and a cultural name for the people who share cultural traits from Puget Sound in Washington State all the way up through to Yakutat Bay. Most of the Native culture you will see in Southeast Alaska is Northwest Coast. The Northwest Coast people are known as the only New World people to have developed a rich and complex culture without the benefit of an agricultural base. During the few months of summer they intensively fished for salmon, eulachon, and herring and gathered wild foods like berries, roots, seaweed and tubers. In the north, sealing added to the subsistence base. The Northwest Coast people were able to accumulate a surplus of food that could be stored for the rest of the year. Now with leisure time they embellished their culture, developing a sophisticated social and political system, expansive oral history, intricate fishing technology, and a tradition of beautifully crafted woodwork and skillful weaving.

Traditionally, Northwest Coast people lived in villages along the beach near fishing rivers or streams. Cedar planked homes known as long houses contained a clan or extended lineage of several families. Fish were harvested by nets, weir, dams and spears. The Northwest Coast people did not hunt whale (the exception being the annual hunt of the Makah in Washington State). Huge dugout canoes were carved primarily for use in trading and raiding. Goods obtained in raids were often used in potlatches.

The Tlingit (Pronounced Kling-kit)

Southeast Alaska is the homeland of the Tlingit. They are one of several tribal groups within the Northwest Coast Culture. The Tlingit are divided into geographic groups extending from Cape Fox in the south to Yakutat in the north. Like all Northwest Coast people the Tlingit are matrilineal, tracing their ancestry through the mother. Because kinship identification is still used among Tlingit today, it is important to understand how this works: every community is internally divided into groups of two. This type of social organization is called a moiety. Each Tlingit moiety is represented by a totemic ancestor; either Eagle or Raven. Tlingit moieties are exogamous, requiring their members to marry outside of their moiety. Ravens must marry eagles, eagles marry ravens. Children take the moiety of their mother. Each moiety is further divided into houses or clans, also represented by totemic ancestors. Within the raven moiety there may be for example, three clans: frog, sea tern and sockeye. The eagles may also have three: wolf, bear, and killer whale. If a man from the Eagle moiety, of the Wolf house marries a Raven, from the Frog house, their children will be Raven/Frog like mom.

Totem Poles

Totem poles were carved for different purposes. They were never worshipped. In a culture with no written language the carvings depicted histories, family lineages, stories, and even important people for all to see. Totem poles include:

Clan pole

Totemic clan figures usually raised outside a clan house.

Greeting poles

Welcome sign identifying the village

House poles

Usually the carved posts inside a clan house

Mortuary pole

Remains of a chief or shaman were placed inside

Honor or shaming pole

Carved to honor or shame an individual

Story pole

Important characters within a myth, legend or history

The Potlatch

A potlatch is an event where distinguished guests are invited to participate in the observation of a significant event like a birth, death, wedding, alliance, rite of passage, or remembrance of an ancestor. It was and still is practiced by Northwest Coast people all along the Pacific Coast from Washington to Alaska. It is a very subtle but effective social, political and economic vehicle of redistribution and balance.

During "the old days" quantity as well as quality was of value in Northwest Coast culture. Clan chiefs would amass large quantities of everything and anything to represent wealth and power. Once an appropriate occasion arose, a potlatch was announced. The potlatch could last for days. Huge bowls specifically carved for the potlatch would be piled high with food; guests would be given lavish gifts. In some extreme cases the host would show his wealth by giving away or destroying his own property. By giving the most extravagant potlatch the host elevates himself within the community; though he exhausts his material wealth he is held in the highest esteem until someone else holds a bigger and better potlatch. Honored guests are expected to reciprocate the invitation by holding their own potlatch within a finite period of time, usually two years. Though the first host may currently be broke, he can expect to receive back goods and gifts several times over by attending future potlatches. Over the years some things have changed within the potlatch ceremony, but the purpose remains the same. Contemporary potlatches are still held to celebrate significant people and events, and guests are still generously served food and showered with gifts.

FACTS

Now the story does not end here; when the children reach puberty and start to learn about their kinship identification --- all the sacred songs and dances and symbols that are proprietary among their group --- dad cannot teach them. Dad does not know. He is from the opposite moiety. In order for his kids to receive the proper education, the most significant male within mom's side of the family, which means her brother or uncle, will be

the teacher. However, it will be dad's responsibility to teach the ways of his moiety to his sister's children, who are also Eagle/Wolf just like him. Whew!

All the songs, dances and designs associated with a family are proprietary and are not shared. They are like brands or crests identifying who is who. Those symbols carved onto a pole and erected in front of ones house were some of the earliest "heraldic poles." Heraldic or clan poles are one of many kinds of totem poles carved and raised by the Northwest Coast people. They are the only Native American culture to carve these types of poles. Artists who paint teepees and totem poles together do not have their Native history straight.

The artistic style of Northwest Coast art is at times difficult to decipher. Elements are depicted in split image or both sides at once, as though they were split down the middle and folded forward. The two motifs that are the most important part of Tlingit iconography are eagle and raven. Ravens, which are as big as some eagles in Alaska, are very smart birds. Eagles are strong. The Tlingit often debate which is it better to be strong or smart?

In the early 20th century, outsiders started coming to the Alaskan territory for many reasons. After the gold rush, canneries were built in the same spot where the Tlingit fished for salmon. With the Canadian Indian Act of 1880, the potlatch, speaking the native language, or carving totem

TERRY'S TIPS

How do you tell eagle from raven in Tlingit art?

Look carefully at the beak. Eagle is depicted with a curved beak, raven's beak is straight.

Raven   *Eagle*

poles became illegal; similar campaigns were launched in the territory of Alaska to acculturate the Tlingit. Children were sent away to Indian schools far from home. Missionaries incorrectly believed totem poles were being worshipped and called the Tlingit idolaters. Without access to their seasonal supply of fish, villages were forced to work in a cash economy. Many people died of disease, and many people left. Those who remained were made to feel their traditional ways were wrong and bad. Many practices, beliefs and dialects died out with the last elder. Anthropologists and photographers came to document what they thought was a disappearing culture. Collectors came and dismantled entire villages. The future looked dim.

In 1934, the territory of Alaska rejected the Wheeler-Howard Act that provided federal land to be set aside for Native Americans. The territory voted for full social, political and economic equality for all Native peoples. Though the belief was still held that full acculturation was the only way Natives would succeed, communities actively participated in local government and elected officials to the territorial legislature. The question of land rights had not yet been addressed but Natives now represented Native interests.

In the 1960's, people of color and ethnicity felt empowered by the events of the Civil Rights Movement. Communities researching their histories proudly started to reclaim their heritage. In Canada, the restrictive Indian Act was repealed in 1951; and potlatch restrictions were eased in Alaska. Despite the fervor in the Lower 48, much had deteriorated in Alaska since traditional lifestyles were censored; when it came to traditional ways many did not know what to do, or who they really were. Little by little communities were reconstructing their past, based upon the fragments of culture remembered by elders or stored in museum vaults. Villages sued to repatriate artifacts and remains from universities and museums. Entire collections were returned. Ethnographies were studied. Puzzle pieces were fit together. One of the greatest catalysts to the revitalization of Tlingit culture in Southeast Alaska has been tourism. With an ever-increasing number of cruise ships calling on Southeast Alaskan ports, Native Americans are able to showcase their culture. For the first time in many generations Tlingit proudly display their totemic emblems and traditional regalia as they share information about their culture with visitors.

The matter of Native land claims in Alaska came to a head in 1967, when a vast amount of oil was discovered in Prudhoe Bay. Fearing that disputed land claims would disrupt or hold back the development of the oil reserves, the state quickly signed the Alaskan Native Claims Settlement

How can you tell if Native art is authentic?

To ensure that Native craftsmen and artists are protected, the state of Alaska issues two types of identification. If you are looking for authentic Alaskan arts and crafts, look for these two symbols. Merchandise marked with the "Silver Hand" which states – Authentic Native Handicraft from Alaska - has been made by Alaskan Inuit, Aleut, Athabascan or Northwest Coast Natives. The "Made in Alaska" sticker with the polar bear means the item has been made by a resident Alaskan artist of any ethnicity.

Act in 1971. Since becoming a territory, Natives claimed rights to over 375 million acres of land. With the Alaskan Native Claims Settlement Act, Alaskan Natives were given 17.8 million hectares of land and one billion dollars. The bill also established Native corporations as owners of the granted land and trustees over the money. In some cases the land and monies have been invested wisely to the long-term benefit of the community; in other cases land has been misused and monies squandered. One of the success stories of the Alaskan Native Claims Settlement Act is the creation of Native owned and operated interpretative centers and tourist venues like Mt. Roberts Tramway in Juneau. Not only is the tramway a financial success, it offers the Tlingit an opportunity to tell their own history.

The Russians

Peter the Great, Czar of Russia, first commissioned the Danish mariner Vitus Bering to determine whether or not Asia and North America were joined. In 1728, he sailed through the strait that now bears his name, but had to turn back due to bad weather. He returned in 1741, this time approaching the North American mainland. Bering himself did not make it back to Russia. His men, however, returned with 800 sea otter pelts and other precious furs, prompting the Russian claim to this part of the New World.

From the Kamchatka Peninsula, Alaska's Attu Island is just 221 miles away. Like stepping stones along a garden path, the Aleutian Island chain easily led the Russians to America. Crossing the Aleutians the Russians encountered the Aleuts, the indigenous residents of the islands. The Aleut were brave warriors but no match for the Russians with their guns and metal swords. The Russians prevailed and forced the Aleuts into slavery, often using them as human shields in battles against other tribal groups. The Russians were not interested in colonization. Their intent was trapping fur-bearing animals. Russia traded fur with China, and the most

57

precious pelts of the time were sea otter. The Russians expanded down the Alaskan coast as far as they found otters. The southernmost Russian outpost in America was located close to present day Mendocino, California.

The first permanent settlement established by the Russian-American Trading Company was on Kodiak Island. Czarist Russia grew very wealthy off Kodiak Island sea otter pelts, hunting the animals to the brink of extinction. In 1799, Alesander Baranof, chief manager, left Kodiak Island to establish a more centrally located community in the south. He founded St. Archangel Michael on what is now Baranof Island. The natives of the island, the Kiksadi Tlingit, heard how cruel the Russians were to the Aleuts, and were not going to allow them to stay. The Tlingit burned the Russian village in 1802. Two years later, Baranof negotiated with the Tlingit to build New Archangel on the site of present day Sitka.

The town of New Archangel was one of the most elegant and wealthy cities of its time. It was called The Paris of the Pacific. Dignitaries detoured north to be wined and dined by Baranof in his sumptuous home high atop Castle Hill. Built in 1837 and known as Baranof's Castle, the structure burned twice before it was demolished. The crowning glory of the community was the Russian Orthodox Church built in 1848. The original St. Michael's church burned in 1966 but was rebuilt using the original plans.

Though things seemed to be going well, the resources of Czar Nicholas were strained after the Crimean War and Russia agreed to sell its American claim to the United States in 1867 for a sum of 7.2 million dollars. That works out to be less than .02 cents an acre! And so ends the Russian occupation of Southeast Alaska.

The Americans

Just as the Russian chapter ends, the United States chapter begins. Secretary of State William Seward believed in the United States' need for expansion and was eager to negotiate the purchase of the Alaskan territory. In 1867, little was known about Alaska and the public perception was that it was all a frozen wasteland. Even though it seemed Seward got a bargain at .02 cents an acre, constituents ridiculed him and called the deal Seward's Folly and Seward's Icebox. Seward had great confidence in the purchase and envisioned that one day the vast land would not only join the Union but be subdivided into several states. No one had any idea what wealth Alaska would hold.

The Americans kept the former Russian town of New Archangel as the first territorial capital, giving it the name Sitka from the Tlingit *shee-atka* for "by the sea." The territory was ruled as a military domain with little interest in the establishment of a formal government. Ten years after the purchase, customs collectors replaced the military and were the only federal representation in the territory. In 1890, the Sitka Times published this article called *Law and Disorder in Alaska*:

> *A murder is committed at Kodiak. A month or two later a sailing vessel arrives. The murder is reported and on its return to San Francisco, word is sent to the Deputy Marshall at Unalaska, also by sailing vessel… which makes semi-annual trips. He then reports to his chief in Sitka, via San Francisco, and…in the course of a year or so, he may get a warrant for the arrest of the malefactor. He will take the first vessel for San Francisco, thence to Kodiak – as this is the shortest and usually only route between ports. If he is lucky enough to find the man still alive, he will arrest him; and… he and his prisoner will wait quietly another six months, when by… way of San Francisco and Puget Sound, prisoner and marshal may arrive at Sitka to find that in the charge of administration, the case has been forgotten.*

Back in Sitka in 1880, a Tlingit chief named Cowee heard there was gold on a creek to the east. Knowing gold was important to the white man, he paid two prospectors to go look. Joe Juneau and Dick Harris set out. After squandering Cowee's money and selling his equipment they returned back empty handed. Cowee was enraged and sent the men back to find the gold and repay the debt. In 1880, Juneau and Harris found gold on a creek they called Gold Creek. However, rather than returning back to Cowee, they packed their pockets and bags with gold and headed for the Canadian border where they were intercepted by the Royal Canadian Mounted Police and sent back to Cowee. As punishment the two men were required to pay back Cowee for his investment plus damages.

Word spread of the strike on Gold Creek and soon a tent city sprang up. Juneau and Harris were famous. As the town grew they wanted to give it a name; Harris felt Harrisburg was fitting, Juneau wanted Juneau. They put it to a vote. The night before, Juneau entertained the voters by plying them with liquor, so the next day, feeling obliged to the generosity of Juneau, they voted in his favor and Juneau became the town's official name. In 1900, the legislative capital was moved to Juneau. In 1912 it became the official territorial and later the state capital.

More gold was being mined out of the mountains of Juneau than anyone ever imagined. However, the strike that really put Alaska on the map didn't even happen in Alaska.

The Klondike Gold Rush

Way up in the Yukon Territory of Canada, in 1896, George Washington Carmack was prospecting with his two Native American brothers-in-law, Skookum Jim and Tagish Charlie. They had been working Rabbit Creek off the Klondike. Lo 'n behold, they found gold – lots of gold! They filled everything they had with gold and made their way to Forty-mile, the closest tent city. Heading straight for the saloon, the lucky prospectors started to brag. Pretty soon you can imagine there was no one left in the bar; they were all on their way to stake their claim on Rabbit Creek. Soon so much gold was being taken from Rabbit Creek that it was called Bonanza Creek. River boats filled with Klondike Gold sailed down the Yukon and out along the coast headed for points south. The first to reach a major city was the *S.S. Portland* that arrived into Seattle in the spring of 1897. Hearing of the Portland's cargo, the Seattle Post-Intelligencer newspaper ran the famous headline GOLD! GOLD! GOLD! People from all over

the country were inspired by rumors of gold nuggets as big as a man's fist. Even the mayor of Seattle quit his job and bought a ticket, North to Alaska!

Accurate information about the trip into the gold fields was hard to come by. Several routes were available; some were long and expensive, while others were unrealistic and dangerous. The most popular way followed a course similar to that of your cruise ship sailing up the Inside Passage to the head of Lynn Canal. From there you could cross the Coast Mountains

The Dead Horse Trail

Outfitters in places like Seattle, Portland, and Vancouver sold naïve wanna-be prospectors supplies that often were not suited for the terrain or conditions. They started rumors that the White Pass was traversable by pack animal in order to sell horses, mules, wagons and carts. Nags destined for the glue factory were bought for a few dollars and sold to the prospectors for 100x the amount. In 1898 over 3,000 horses died on the White Pass, giving it the nickname the Dead Horse Trail.

by way of two mountain passes that would then lead to a series of lakes and rivers leading to the Klondike. It sounded easy – but it wasn't. Out of the tent city of Skagway you could cross via the 43 mile White Pass. From nearby Dyea, the Chilkoot Pass was shorter in length – about 33 miles - but steeper and more treacherous with an icy summit of 3,700 feet.

In the summer of 1898, over 30,000 people were camped out on the mud-flats of Skagway and Dyea. Thugs like Jefferson "Soapy" Smith tyrannized the town. Life was tough. Knowing that most who were seeking their fame and fortune in the Yukon would not survive a Canadian winter without proper preparation, the Royal Canadian Mounted Police required that everyone entering into Canada be provisioned with one year's worth of supplies. That amounted to one ton of goods. All provisions were account-ed for in full at the border before one was allowed to proceed. That meant in most cases instead of making one arduous trip up and over either the White or Chilkoot Pass, prospectors wanting to enter Canada had to pack in their goods, making up to 42 trips before their "outfit" was complete. Unfortunately, by the time the few people who completed the trek actu-ally arrived, all the claims were taken. It had been two years since Car-mack discovered gold; most of the miners who were already in the area staked claims. Of the 100,000 who set out only 30,000 made it, and most of them had to work for someone else, do something else, or go home. It is estimated that 22 million dollars in gold was taken out of the Klondike in two years, but only about 300 prospectors "struck it rich." Much of the flavor of the Gold Rush is still preserved in the town of Skagway where 14 buildings are on the National Historic Register, including the Arctic Brotherhood and the Assayer's Office.

Gold continued to be the mainstay of the Alaskan economy from 1900 until 1945, when the A & J Mine closed in Juneau. There is still plenty of gold to be mined in Alaska but cost effective ways of getting at it have yet to be found. One of the most recent gold mines to re-open in the state is the Kensington Mine located 45 minutes northwest of Juneau on the east side of Lynn Canal. Today, however, there is another type of gold -- black gold – that has become the state's primary source of income, surpassing fishing and timber.

World War II

Since the close of the Gold Rush not much attention was paid to Alaska. In 1932, the population of the territory was 72,524. Over 60% of the people were Natives living in remote villages. The area lacked infrastructure and was virtually undefended. One railroad linked Seward, Anchorage and Fairbanks, and a highway ran between Valdez and Fairbanks. A small garrison was stationed at Fort William Seward south of Skagway. With rumblings of war, Congress was reminded, "Whosoever controls Alaska, controls the North Pacific." After Germany invaded Poland in 1939, funds were appropriated to build up Alaska's coastal defense and within no time naval stations were constructed throughout Southeast and Southcentral Alaska in Sitka, Dutch Harbor, Anchorage and Kodiak; but with no access how would they defend the interior and far north? No road or rail system existed. In eight short months, working from March through November 1942, thousands of United States and Canadian troops headed north to build the 1,200 mile Alaska-Canadian Highway or Alcan Highway; carved out of remote wilderness, it was called, "The highway that could not be built."

That did not stop the Japanese. In 1942 they bombed Dutch Harbor and occupied two islands in the Aleutians, Attu and Kiska. The battle to take the desolate island of Attu killed 2,600 Japanese soldiers and 549 American troops, the second bloodiest battle of the war in the Pacific after Iwo Jima.

The Aleut Evacuation

Fearing occupation of the Aleutian Islands thousands of Native Aleuts were taken from their homes and relocated to Southeast Alaska where they were forced to live in dilapidated fish canneries. Far removed from the open treeless environment of their island homes, they became ill in the dark, damp land of Southeast Alaska. With no doctors, no running water and no sanitation, hundreds died. After the war almost no original buildings stood. Houses were ransacked and burned and churches were plundered. No apologies were made. Years later, as part of the restitution for the internment of Japanese-Americans as well as the Aleuts, the United States government compensated both groups and issued them a formal apology through the enactment of the 1988 Civil Liberties Act .

FACTS

MAKING A LIVING IN SOUTHEAST ALASKA

The war effort paved the way for statehood. On January 3, 1959, Alaska became the 49th state of the United States of America. Many servicemen remained in Alaska. Former air bases turned into airports and the military transport system carved out of the interior became the Alcan Highway. Anchorage and Fairbanks, formerly small railroad towns, boomed. Isolated communities in Southeast were served by a comprehensive ferry system.

Alaska's economy has been tied to periods of boom and bust. Covering such a vast area, the state is rich in resources but low on capital. Due to the limited number of people and cash available to exploit these resources, for years the economy has been driven by outside interests from J.P. Morgan to British Petroleum. Along the coast of Southeast Alaska, major industries also rely upon non-Alaskan companies and have been subject to their own ups and downs.

Fishing

Commercial fishing, packing, and canning have been one of the most important industries in Southeast Alaska since the area was first settled. Commercial fishermen, most of whom still are independent operators, rely upon the annual salmon migration along with herring, rockfish, halibut and crab. Over-fishing and international boundary disputes have affected recent harvests, as have issues of waste management and dumping. The recent interest in the health benefits of wild salmon has caused an increase in profits among many local fishermen.

Commercial fishing is one of the most important industries in the state of Alaska. In Southeast, your cruise ship will be sharing the water with many different types of commercial fishing vessels. There are gill-netters, purse seiners, trollers, and long liners. Many of the smaller, privately owned boats bring in their catch each day. Others off-load onto larger vessels especially equipped to flash freeze the catch for freshness. In town, you will probably be able to find fishermen along the docks. Time permitting, they are always willing to share a fish story or two.

Timber

One of the largest industries in Southeast Alaska has been timber and pulp. Stricter regulations on logging, controls on emissions of mills, and the cost of timber have shut down many operations. The cost of doing business in the timber industry in Alaska has made the price of lumber imported from Washington State less expensive than locally produced wood.

The closure of mills has severely affected many towns in Southeast.

Oil

Though Southeast Alaskans are not directly involved in oil production, the entire state is affected by oil as the largest sector of the economy. Over 25% of the crude oil produced in the United States comes from Alaska. In 1967, the economy of Alaska boomed again with the discovery of vast reserves of oil under the North Slope. To get that oil to an ice-free port for transport required moving it from Prudhoe Bay to Valdez. Traveling over miles of permafrost, one of the biggest challenges engineers faced was how to keep the warm oil flowing through the pipe from melting the ground beneath. The answer was a system of looped tubes filled with liquid ammonia imbedded in each of the hundreds of above ground pipeline supports. Through continuous heat exchange from the circulating ammonia, the heat produced by the 120 degree Fahrenheit oil is dissipated, keeping the permafrost at normal temperatures. (Thanks for that explanation go to a guest who was an engineer who worked on the design of the pipeline. I could never have told you that!)

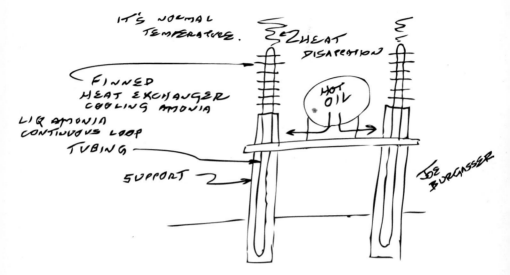

Since starting up in 1977, the 800 mile long Trans Alaska Pipeline moves 1.2 million barrels of oil a day. Located in Southcentral Alaska, many cruise ships call upon the port of Valdez.

Exxon Valdez Oil Spill

How are things going in Prince William Sound since the 1989 spill dumped 13 million gallons of crude oil over this environmentally sensitive area? Puddles of weathered oil are still found under rocks along the beach. Though nature is resilient, populations of marine mammals and commercial fish have yet to reach pre-1989 levels. One of the best things to come out of this disastrous mess, however, is stricter control and regulation on commercial vessels, including cruise ships. Multi-million dollar fines are automatically charged to any company in violation of these new rules.

FACTS

Tourism

Alaska's current economic boom is in tourism. Revenues have now exceeded both fishing and timber. Arriving primarily on cruise ships, more than 2.5 million visitors will come to Southeast Alaska this summer. For ailing communities struck by unemployment from declining fishing and timber, tourism has provided an infusion of cash into the economy. Local areas and attractions are receiving a much needed boost. Residents have learned to commodify local arts, crafts, and culture into marketable merchandise for the visitor.

THE SPIRIT OF THE FRONTIER

Living in the Last Frontier makes Alaskans a hardy bunch. It takes a certain kind of person to knowingly pull up stakes and head north. In the midst of a long, cold winter there are many who question if it was worth it. However, once the long days of summer set in, all is forgotten.

Most of Alaska's population is clustered around the Pacific coast where temperatures rarely fall to the extremes experienced in the interior. As of 2010, Alaska's largest city is Anchorage, population 279,243; followed by Fairbanks, population 97,000; and Juneau, the state capital, population 30,980. Temperatures in Southeast Alaska are especially comfortable with averages that range from summer highs in the mid 60's to winter lows in the mid 30's. Did you know that Juneau's average temperatures are warmer than both Chicago and Minneapolis? Though Southeast does not receive much snow, it does get a lot of rain. Ketchikan is the rain capital of the United States with its 162 inches a year. Lucky for you, villages like Little Port Walker are not on the cruise circuit – it gets an average of 225 inches of rain. According to climatologists studying Alaska, the state is warming faster than any other place on the planet.

Alaska in the summer is a paradise for hiking, fishing, boating and outdoor fun. Due to its northern location, on June 21st, the longest day, Southeast Alaskans can enjoy 19 hours of daylight. It is very hard to pull yourself away from the spectacular views that go on into the wee hours when most of us folks from the "Lower Pasture" should be sleeping. Alaskans, like the wildlife, seem to have adapted and make use of every ray of sunlight. You will see people picnicking and playing baseball at 11 pm!

For those of you who have come to Alaska in hope of seeing the Aurora Borealis or Northern Lights, unfortunately mid-summer is not the best time. The aurora starts to be visible in late August as the night sky grows darker. Swathes of iridescent light caused by sunspot activity ebb and flow silently across the night sky. During solar storms charged particles are thrown into space and pulled into the earth's atmosphere concentrating at the poles. Like neon in a tube these particles glow with varying color and intensity. Though solar storms happen year-round, these beautiful displays are only seen under clear, dark skies. These beautiful displays also occur in the southern hemisphere as well where they are called the Aurora Australis.

Life in Southeast Alaska is very different from not only the Lower 48, but the rest of the state. With the exception of Skagway and Haines, all the cities, towns, and villages are accessible only by air or sea. That's right. Located on islands or isolated mainland areas, you cannot drive to Ketchikan, Juneau, Sitka, Wrangell, Petersburg, etc. You must come and go by jet, seaplane, private plane, ferry, private boat, or barge! That includes not only people but things, as well. Your car, furniture, groceries and mail are all dependent on air or sea transport. If there is a bad storm – no one gets anything. People must be well prepared and very resourceful as there are times when these communities do get temporarily cut-off. Juneau is the only state capital (on the mainland) to which you cannot drive. Some island communities are so small and isolated that kids are taken to school on school boats.

Because of the reliance on air and sea transportation, Alaska has more private pilot's licenses on a per capita base than any other state. In Southeast Alaska, where there are so few miles of road, kids often learn to fly before they learn to drive.

Will we be able to see the Northern Lights?

Your best chance of seeing the Northern Lights in Southeast Alaska is late summer/early fall (late August/early September through April/May). Best time is between 11pm – 1am. If solar storms have taken place, watch the northern horizon. The aurora appears as a ghostly glow that intensifies and fades. These fingers of light can be green, white, blue or pink in color. Remember that you need a clear as well as dark sky – that means no clouds, which can get tricky in Southeast Alaska. In extreme cases the aurora may be visible in Southeast Alaska if the auroral index is 4 or greater. To check the index, go to the University of Alaska's Geophysical Institute's website for an up-to-the-minute auroral forecast.

www.gedds.alaska.edu/AuroraForecast

The blue hulled ferries plying the waters of Southeast and Southcentral
Alaska are an indispensable part of life. Affectionately known as the "blue
canoes," the ferries transport people, cars and cargo into small towns and
remote communities all along the coast. Started in 1949 as a private company out of Haines, Steve Homer, Ray Gellote and Robert Sommers purchased an old Navy landing craft and turned her into the *M/V Chilkoot*.
She initially serviced Haines and Juneau. The ferry was a success providing
many with their only connection to the outside world. Hearing how popular and necessary the ferry was to isolated communities, the territorial
government bought the rights and expanded the service, adding the *M/V
Chilkat*. When Alaska became a state in 1959, it was eligible for federal
highway funds. With most of the state's population living on islands in
Southeast, a land highway was not of immediate importance. Instead the
allocation was given to the ferry system, and in 1963 it became known as
the Alaskan Marine Highway System. In 2005, the Marine Highway was
designated one of the 126 Scenic Byways in the United States. Today the

ferries call on 30 ports in Alaska plus Prince Rupert, B.C. and Bellingham, WA. There are now eleven vessels which are all named after glaciers. Before its retirement, the *M/V Bartlett* was the only ferry named after a person; it was named for long-time U.S. Senator E.L. Bartlett. You can board the Alaskan state ferry in Bellingham, Washington and take it as far north Seward. During limited summer service ferries continue to the Aleutians.

Some people choose to live in Alaska because it one of the few places left

in the United States – maybe the world – where one can live a true frontier life. There are individuals and families who prefer to live in the bush. They have none of the modern conveniences. They live off the land. With a subsistence hunting license, they can hunt and fish as needed. Small summer plots yield fresh vegetables that can be preserved. Roots and berries are gathered. Contact with the outside world is limited to two-way radios and the bi-annual visit of the bush pilots. However, recently (some) bush families are known to have made concessions to the outside world by installing solar panels, generators and satellite dishes.

The popular statistic that there are many more men in Alaska to women is still true; estimates are about 2 men to every 1 woman. However, as many Alaskan women will tell you, *"The odds are good, but the goods are odd!"*

Alaska has no state tax. There are borough taxes. The cost of living is high due to the fact almost all goods and materials must be imported. Wages are adjusted for the higher cost of living.

One of the benefits of living in Alaska is your annual check from the Permanent Fund. Established in 1976 and implemented in 1982, the Permanent Fund is the redistribution of dividends earned from state mineral rights. Checks are sent to all eligible residents who have lived in the state for more than two years. Permanent fund checks can range from a few hundred dollars to a few thousand.

...a word about mosquitoes

Alaska is known for mosquitoes, very big mosquitoes at that. Most of the tall tales of mosquitoes carrying away small dogs are not true! In Southeast Alaska, mosquitoes come out in June. Most people say if you are camping or walking in the woods, June is the worst time. The rest of the year, mosquitoes are not a problem unless you go into deeply wooded areas. If you are planning a good hike on a mountain trail it is still advisable to wear repellant.

FACTS

As a young state, Alaska has been going through its own growing pains. A few years back, people started talking about moving the capital. Originally, the territorial capital was Sitka, but when gold was discovered outside of what is now Juneau, the capital was moved. Now most of the people live in or near Anchorage, so wouldn't it make sense to move the capital where all the people are? In 1974, the people voted on moving the capital but not until they also reassessed all the state symbols to make sure they still were appropriate as well.

They looked at the state flag. Everyone loved the flag. The flag was designed by a 13 year old Aleut boy, Benny Benson. Benny was going to school in Seward and lived at the Jesse Lee Home. He entered his design in the territorial flag competition in 1926. Of the 142 entries, he won! Benny put the Big Dipper on the flag and said Ursus Major, The Great Bear, signified the strength of Alaska. He also put the North Star on the flag to represent Alaska, as he hoped one day it would become the northernmost state. He used the yellow for the gold of Alaska on a background of blue for the night sky. No one wanted to change the flag.

The state tree is the Sitka spruce, a tall, majestic tree liked by everyone.. The state flower is the forget-me-not, with a beautiful, fragrant little bloom that everyone loves. No change there. The state fish is the king salmon; who can argue with that? The state mineral is gold, of course! But the state bird is the willow ptarmigan. Now the willow ptarmigan is a member of the grouse family; it changes its plumage to camouflage season-ally, but it is not very smart. Some say it makes a turkey look clever. So, during the vote, there were some who felt a more appropriate state bird would be the mosquito. Needless to say Juneau is still the capital and the ptarmigan is still the state bird. Oh, life in The Last Frontier!

What's happening in Southeast?

Summer is the season for locals to kick up their heels. With those lovely long summer days you'll see people out enjoying themselves at all hours. This is the time for fairs and festivals celebrating just about anything; essentially it's an excuse to have a party. If you are in the right place at the right time you may be lucky enough to attend:

Sealaska Heritage Institute Celebration - This biennial gathering of all Tlingit, Haida and Tsimshian people takes place in June in Juneau. Started in 1982, as an opportunity to "showcase and celebrate Southeast Alaska Native culture and traditions," it has grown into an anticipated event for the community. It is open to the public; admission allows you to see participants in full regalia performing Native songs, dances, narrations and storytelling. There are juried competitions. There is also an art fair where you can see and purchase everything from hand beadwork to paintings and sculpture. There is always food and you won't want to miss real hot smoked salmon.

Alaska State Fair - Held at the end of summer in Palmer, this is the place to see all those huge Matanuska cabbages and pumpkins. In addition to farm exhibits, pies and amusement rides, the state fair is known for beautiful textiles, quilts, woodworking and other ingenious by-products of frontier resourcefulness.

World Eskimo-Indian Olympic Games - Held in July, indigenous people from all parts come to Fairbanks to take part in the WEIO. The Inuit or "Eskimo" People extend all around the Arctic Circle, so contestants come from Canada, Siberia and Finland! Some of the events in which they participate are amazing – mostly based around skills originally needed for the hunt.

Pennock Island Swim Challenge - If you don't have anything better to do, you might want to start training now for the August swim around Pennock Island. Participants swim the 8.2 miles around the island west of Ketchikan in 50° water. Brrrrr!

Moose Dropping Festival - According to the Talkeetna Chamber of Commerce - where the event is held - the festival is, "Mountain Mother contest, one-pitch softball, free music and entertainment, and moose poop falling from the sky." Aah yes - not to be missed.

Independence Day Run - Every 4th of July runners from around the world gather in Seward to scale the 3,022 foot Mt. Marathon. The record time up and back is currently 43 minutes, 39 seconds. My best time is just under three hours not including lunch!

6 ALASKA IS "THE GREAT LAND" FOR ITS FABULOUS, FRESH FOOD

Summer in Alaska means long days of ripening fruits and berries, harvests of gigantic garden vegetables, and baskets of seafood caught fresh daily – the makings from which celebrated chefs and creative camp cooks fashion fabulous feasts to match the magnificent land from which it comes. Up here people take their food seriously; you gotta have a hardy, nutritious meal when it's 40° below. The taste of Alaska incorporates many flavors and traditions from the Native population to the pioneers and prospectors that settled in The Last Frontier.

The original inhabitants of Southeast Alaska, the Tlingit, knew every plant, bird, fish and animal of the forest and sea and used them judiciously for food, medicine and ceremony. Along with salmon, halibut and eulachon, they harvested seaweed, berries, herring eggs, seagull eggs and seal. The first Europeans were Russian and with them they introduced piroshki, spiced tea and hearty borscht. Following the Alaska Purchase, prospectors by the thousands were lured by the promise of gold. Trekking over the treacherous terrain they brought sourdough starter for quick cakes and bread. Together they form the cuisine of the region.

Taku Lodge

What could be so special about a day trip for lunch? Well, if you are going to Taku Lodge outside of Juneau, you are in for a treat. With Taku Glacier in the front yard the location is breathtaking. Built in 1923, the lodge has been many things and has seen its share of colorful characters. After taking in the sights enjoy fresh grilled salmon, biscuits, coleslaw and a selection of beer and wine chilled on glacial ice. An added bonus is the chance to see the black bears that regularly come down to clean the grill. You've heard of licking the bowl; these guys climb up on the barbecue to lick the grill, and many have the scars to prove it.

SEAFOOD

Southeast Alaska is known for its seafood. Halibut, herring, trout, and, of course, salmon dominate most restaurant menus. Wild Alaskan salmon has become very popular in recent years due to studies on its nutritional value as an excellent source of Omega 3 oils. Whether you like the stronger taste of Sockeye or the mild and meaty King, there is a salmon for everyone. One of the most authentic ways to serve salmon in Alaska is by hot smoking. This technique for curing salmon has been used for centuries by the Northwest Coast Culture. It uses a hot smokehouse and flavorful woods like alder and apple. You will find hot smoked salmon from Southeast Alaska all the way down to Puget Sound in Washington State. Today connoisseurs produce new exotic flavors using different woods as well as herbs and spices.

From the sea also come shellfish like king crab, Dungeness crab, shrimp and scallops as well as mollusks, including razor clams, littleneck clams, oysters, mussels and geoduck.

TIPS

Gone fishing for the day?

Many cruise ships allow you to bring back your day's catch for the chef to prepare for you and your guests. Ask about such arrangements onboard your ship.

LOCAL PRODUCE

Southeast Alaska is known for its beautiful and bountiful gardens. Long summer days give fruits and vegetables time to truly ripen on the vine. In places like the Matanuska Valley outside of Anchorage in the central, southwest portion of the state, the record for the largest cabbage is 106 pounds! But summer in Alaska also means wild things, like berries. Armed with buckets and pails, locals are serious about their picking. Wild berries are so coveted in some communities that prime patches are "reserved." In Southeast Alaska there are about 50 types of edible berries. You will find wild blueberries, strawberries, blackberries, raspberries, lingonberries, highbush cranberries, currents, huckleberries, cloudberries, and salmon-

berries --and the list goes on. They are made into jams, jellies, syrup, pies, cakes, ice cream and even wine. Hint: A jar of locally made preserves makes a great gift that won't go to waste.

Another delicacy from the forests of Southeast Alaska is mushrooms. There are hundreds of species that grow "like mushrooms" everywhere. Gourmand mycophiles - aka mushroomers - patiently wait for the delicate morels and boletus. However, just as it takes an experienced eye to spot the right berries, it is even more important to know your mushrooms. If you would like to learn more about both berry picking and mushroom hunting, please pick up a good reference book with color photographs and study it carefully.

Hungry?

If you could not get enough of Alaska's fresh, wild salmon or juicy Fruits of the Forest pie, noted international chef Mike Römhild has prepared a selection of his favorite Alaskan recipes for you to try at home. Turn to be page 231 for Chef Mike's "Taste of Alaska."

TIPS

GAME

For many in Alaska the seasonal hunt is not a sport but survival. Deer, caribou, elk, and moose shot in the summer will be stored for many meals to come. Over the years resourceful people living in remote locations have learned to be very creative, coming up with recipes for everything from rabbit ragout to moose meatloaf. If you have an adventurous palate, why not try some sausage, jerky, or canned stew made from wild Alaskan game? It's available.

What will I see while I'm in Alaska?

Most of your time onboard will be spent sailing through the Inside Passage; to make of the most of this valuable time, the next few chapters will look at what can be seen from your ship as you explore Southeast Alaska and the Inside Passage!

TIPS

DAY BY DAY
GUIDE TO CRUISING
ALASKA'S INSIDE PASSAGE

PART 2

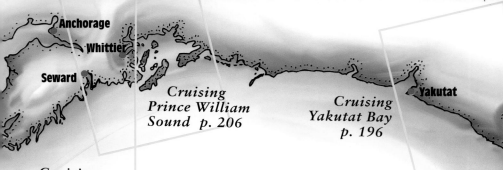

Anchorage

Whittier

Seward

Cruising
Prince William
Sound p. 206

Cruising
Yakutat Bay
p. 196

Yakutat

Cruising
The Gulf of Alaska
p. 216

CRUISING THE
INSIDE PASSAGE

Key for all Maps

●   City or Town

●   Abandoned Town

●   Point of Interest

☐   Detail of Map

◙   Mountain Peak

⊥   International Border

| 200 mi |
| 200 km | Scale |

Skagway

Juneau

Sitka

Ketchikan

Vancouver

Continued on page 98

N
W **E**
S

50 mi
50 km

Bella Bella
pg. 106

*Pulteney Point
Lighthouse*

Port
McNeil

Alert
Bay

*Robson
Bight*

*Seymour
Narrows*
pg. 108

**Campbell
River**

49° 21' N

PACIFIC OCEAN

COAST MOUNTAINS

Vancouver
Island

Georgia Strait

Vancouver

Strait of Juan De Fuca

Victoria

Bellingham

CASCADE MOUNTAINS

OLYMPIC
MOUNTAINS

Bremerton

Seattle

10' W

CITIES AND TOWNS

SEATTLE, WASHINGTON

Coordinates:	47° 36' N, 122° 20' W
Population (2009):	Metropolitan area - 602,374
	Greater Seattle - 3,355,847

It is probably not fair to write about the city you call "home." One's bias is bound to show; but what can you do when your home town is the most beautiful city in the country?

Nestled on the eastern shore of Puget Sound, Seattle is protected from the bad weather off the Pacific, and despite being located further north than Maine, enjoys a mild year-around climate because of the warm North Pacific Current (or Japanese Current). From the city (on a clear day) you can see the snow covered Olympic Mountains to the west and the Cascades to the east. Looming on the southwest horizon is the guardian of the city, 14,411-foot Mt. Rainier. Locals rejoice at its sight, and long-time residents never tire of remarking when, "the mountain is out!" Truly clear

days here are a limited commodity, although not as rare as most visitors imagine. Seattle has a Mediterranean-style climate in that most of the rain falls November to March, while July through September are almost drought-like, giving Seattle an average of about 37 inches of rain a year, considerably less than New York City. Rain falls by the bucketful (more than 140 inches a year) on the western slopes of the Olympic Mountains, producing the Olympic Temperate Rainforest, part of Olympic National Rainforest. The moist air moves east over Puget Sound where it can sit for days, weeks, and months before accumulating enough moisture to actually rain and move on over the Cascades. The moist air then continues over the mountains and is trapped by the Cascades Range, leaving dark clouds that hang over Puget Sound for days, before finally falling as mist, drizzle, spit, showers, rain, etc. The locals are reputed to have as many words for rain as the Inuit for snow. Consequently, Seattle gets more gray days than the neighboring cities of Portland and Vancouver, B.C., although they receive more rainfall. In those cities rain falls, moves on, and the weather clears. In Seattle the clouds just sit there. However, when it DOES clear, it is the most exhilaratingly beautiful city in which to live.

This area of the Pacific Northwest marks the southernmost extent of the Northwest Coast Native American culture. The people who lived here prior to the Europeans were Coast Salish, relatives of the people around Vancouver B.C. The name Seattle comes from the Suquamish chief, Chief Sealth. The city was founded in 1851 by the Denny Party that landed in what is now West Seattle on Alki Point. The community was moved east to its present location on the shores of Elliott Bay. Within a few years it was a bustling mill town and finally in 1893 the terminus of the transcontinental Great Northern railroad. To the great disappointment of Seattle's founding fathers the first transcontinental railroad to serve Puget Sound, the Northern Pacific, chose Tacoma for its terminus in 1873.

Seattle has always had an inextricable tie to Alaska dating back to July 17, 1897, when the steamship Portland sailed into Elliott Bay with two tons of Klondike gold. It was on that day when the Seattle Post-Intelligencer ran the headline "GOLD! GOLD! GOLD!" that men and women started to flock to Seattle in preparation for their trips north to Alaska. Prospectors bought provisions from Seattle merchants in what is now Pioneer Square. To commemorate this historic relationship, many buildings in Pioneer Square are included as part of the Klondike Gold Rush National Monument. Tours are available.

Seattle is still the primary port for provisioning the state of Alaska. Goods are sent up by barge or cargo plane. The Alaska Marine Highway ferry

Seattle's Underground:

Did you know that looming under the streets of historic Pioneer Square is the remnant of another city? No? Well up until 1954, most Seattleites didn't either - not until Bill Speidel wrote a letter to The Seattle Times asking about the authenticity of rumors that the present day city had been built upon the ruins of what was left after The Great Fire of 1889. The response that followed prompted lawmakers to designate the area a historic site, which started the process of preserving the oldest part of the city. What Speidel found continues to fascinate locals and visitors to this day: a series of tunnels that take you past what were the store fronts, hotel lobbies and saloons of Old Seattle. The 1890 fire destroyed 25 blocks of buildings constructed almost entirely of wood. It was vowed that in the future all new structures would be built of stone or brick. Though the buildings were now safer the city was still plagued by poor roads; seepage from Puget Sound and poor drainage from the rain created muddy roads that were reported to have swallowed dogs and children. Eight-foot retaining walls were built along the sides of the mucky roads; the old streets were then filled in and paved over creating new eight foot tall roads. A gap up to 35 feet wide was created between the raised road and the buildings. Ground level front doors and display windows were in the shadow of the eight-foot wall. From the new roads pedestrians crossed the chasm by way of bridges that entered on the second floor, making the original first floor obsolete except for use as a basement. Eventually sidewalks straddled the gap and second floors became first floors, hiding the original storefronts and doorways until their rediscovery in 1954. Today you can explore the original store fronts and buildings of Old Seattle on the Underground Tour. Tickets and tours start at 608 First Avenue in Pioneer Square.

system starts just a few miles north in Bellingham. Like Alaska, Seattle's economy has been predicated on fishing and timber, with its own unique periods of boom and bust. Aircraft manufacturer and long-time Seattle family, Boeing has been responsible for the city's growth in the mid-twentieth century. The Museum of Flight at Boeing Field in south Seattle is a must-see for any aviation enthusiast, as is the Future of Flight Aviation Center at Paine Field in South Everett where you can also tour the largest building in the world (by volume) and see the production lines for the Boeing 747, 767, 777, and the 787.

Seattle still is the Gateway to Alaska. Just as in 1898, visitors are lining the piers of Seattle eager to board ships bound for Alaska. These days a few things have changed - the ships are little more comfortable and the voyage is the destination - but the sentiment remains the same – North to Alaska! In recent years, Seattle has responded to the growing interest in Alaska cruises by building new cruise terminals. Hoping passengers will take advantage of the convenience of travel and the discounts afforded by round-trip domestic airfare, the Port of Seattle has aggressively sought to lure ships to its shores. Located at Pier 66 on Alaskan Way, the Bell Street Terminal was the first to open. With a sweeping view of downtown Seattle and the Olympic Mountains, the terminal is easy walking distance to the city's most popular attractions. Located at the north end of the waterfront, Terminal 91 at Smith Cove is the newest facility; this state-of-the-art cruise terminal located at the base of Magnolia Hill offers new passengers a terminal with a comfortable check-in area, an easy access pick-up area with a thoughtful canopy just in case it rains, ample parking, and taxi vouchers for those departing from Pier 66.

What can you see in a few hours? Depending on where your ship is docked along Alaskan Way, the Seattle Aquarium and pier side shops and restaurants are not far. The aquarium contains exhibits featuring the undersea world of Puget Sound, including a working salmon ladder. The free vintage trolley run that used to service Pier 54 to Pioneer Square has been replaced indefinitely by a free bus run, Route 99. Look for the green and yellow buses painted to look like the old trolleys and printed on their sides with the words "Waterfront Streetcar Line." Seattle Metro also offers free bus service between 6 a.m. and 7 p.m. daily in Downtown Seattle except for Metro routes 116, 118, and 119. The Ride Free Area (RFA) extends from the north at Battery St. to S. Jackson St. on the south, and east at 6th Avenue to the waterfront on the west.

World famous Pike Place Market is located uptown. You can take a taxi or walk from the Bell Street Terminal. To make it easy, there is an elevator from Alaskan Way as well as stairs for the more ambitious. The Market was founded in 1907 and is one of the oldest continuously operating public markets in the country. It is known for its displays of fresh vegetable and flowers, and of course, the "flying" fish! Watch your head as vendors

The Seattle Art Museum Olympic Sculpture Garden

A must for any visitor to the city, the Seattle Art Museum Olympic Sculpture garden was once an industrial eyesore. Today it has been transformed into an oasis of inspiration, a unique blend of art and nature featuring the work of premier contemporary sculpture artists set against a backdrop of the city to the east and Puget Sound and the Olympic Mountains to the west. The Seattle Art Museum awarded the project to the New York based team of Weiss/Manfredi, whose design created a space that supported art, recreation and the local ecosystem. Whether you enjoy the sculpture, fly a kite or just have a tranquil respite in the middle of the city, the Sculpture Garden awaits you. From the Bell Street Terminal take the Waterfront Streetcar north; there is parking nearby if you have a car. Admission to the Sculpture Garden is free.

Why can't cruise ships sail from Seattle straight to Alaska?

A hot topic within the cruise industry is the relevance of a 1917 law called the Jones Act. The Jones Act states that vessels used to transport cargo and passengers between two U.S. ports must be built in the United States, owned by U.S. citizens and manned by U.S. crew. The need for this type of law came about after the Civil War as a way of protecting U.S. cabotage. Unfortunately, today almost all cruise vessels are foreign flag carriers, and therefore they are not permitted to operate exclusively within U.S. waters – a foreign port must be included. Cruise ships embarking guests in Seattle must make a stop at a Canadian port before disembarking the same guests back in Seattle or another US port. This is why for years Alaskan cruises have started in Vancouver – to fulfill the Jones Act. Also, because of the Jones Act, passengers cannot embark and disembark a non-U.S. cruise ship exclusively within Alaska. Penalties for doing so run between $400 - $1000 a person.

are known to startle visitors with a tossed fish or two. The market also offers Market Heritage Tours and Savor Seattle "Chef Tours" featuring local fish and produce; inquire at the Information Booth located at 1st & Pike. Local artists display their wares in stalls both inside and out. And for you nostalgic types, you can visit the very first Starbucks. Aaaww…

Not far away is the downtown and commercial district. Westlake Mall provides covered shopping as well as a chance to hop on the Monorail, the retro, light-rail transport that was built during the 1961 World's Fair. The Monorail will take you to the Seattle Center, home of the World's Fair and the Space Needle, icon of the city. The futuristic 520 foot tower has a restaurant and observation area for a breathtaking 360° view. The Seattle Center is also home of the Pacific Science Center which, with its interactive exhibits, is a great place to take the kids. And for all you Baby Boomers don't forget Paul Allen's Experience Music Project, Science Fiction Museum and Hall of Fame.

If you prefer history and culture, walk from the Pike Place Market south down 1st Avenue to the newly expanded Seattle Art Museum. The museum is known in particular for its collection of Asian and African art as well as some fine pieces from the Northwest School. Much of the Asian Art, however, is at SAM's original museum in Volunteer Park on Capitol Hill not far from the grave of Bruce Lee in Lake View Cemetery. You will need a short taxi ride to visit this location. To encourage more people to visit the Art Museum and the Asian Art Museum, SAM offers the following free admission program each month. Entry is free to everyone the first Thursday, free to seniors (62+) the first Friday, and free to teens (13 – 19 with ID) the second Friday. If you are interested in architecture you may want to continue south to Pioneer Square with its historic buildings, cafes and galleries. Not too far away is the International District; this is Seattle's "Chinatown" and is filled with Asian shops and restaurants.

If you have never been through the Panama Canal, you may want to see the Hiram Chittenden Locks and Fish Ladder. Built 1911, these chambered locks raise and lower boats between the freshwater of Lake Union and the saltwater of Puget Sound using the same technology as the Panama Canal. The 21-step fish ladder has underwater viewing windows to watch salmon returning to spawn from June through November. This is also the time to look for savvy sea lions. With so much to see the Ballard Locks, as they are known, is a fun spot for a picnic. However, if you are in the mood for something special, continue to nearby Shilshoe Marina and experience the breathtaking sunset views at some of the city's best seafood restaurants.

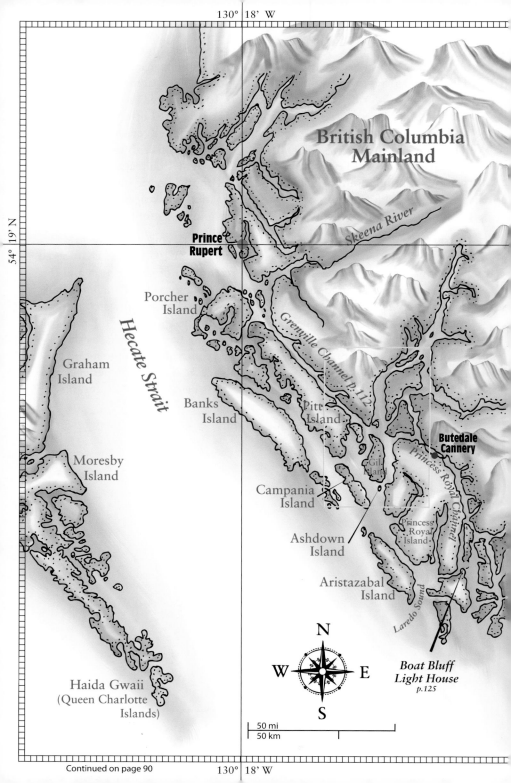

54° 19' N

British Columbia
Mainland

Skeena River

Prince Rupert

Porcher Island

Hecate Strait

Grenville Channel p.112

Graham Island

Banks Island

Pitt Island

Gil Island

Butedale Cannery

Moresby Island

Princess Royal Channel

Campania Island

Ashdown Island

Princess Royal Island

Aristazabal Island

Laredo Sound

Haida Gwaii
(Queen Charlotte Islands)

N
W E
S

Boat Bluff Light House
p.125

50 mi
50 km

Continued on page 90

VANCOUVER, BRITISH COLUMBIA

Coordinates: 49° 21′ N, 123° 10′ W

Population (2009):   Metropolitan area - 640,000

                          Greater Vancouver - 2,216,965

Vancouver is the largest city in British Columbia, the third largest in Canada after Toronto and Montreal and the country's largest and most important port. Greater Vancouver has a current population of over 2 million. It has the most dense and diversified urban population outside of New York. Divided by Vancouver Harbor, the city has grown around beautiful sheltered coves and inlets. Vancouver is proud of its ethnically diverse population and its spirit of inclusion. The city is divided into colorful and distinctive neighborhoods; Vancouver's Chinatown has the second largest Asian population outside of Asia (San Francisco being Number One). Vancouver was home to the 2010 Winter Olympics and the 1986 World's Fair called, "Expo." The cruise terminal at Canada Place was the Canadian Pavilion during the Fair. The roof was designed to look like billowing sails of a Spanish galleon. As many as five cruise ships can dock at Canada Place. Next door, the red, white and blue ferries you see plying the harbor are Sea Buses; they connect downtown Vancouver and North Vancouver. Each Sea Bus can carry 400 people and makes the trip in 15 minutes. Not far away is the SkyTrain, Vancouver's rapid transit system that loops around this fabulous city.

George Vancouver first sailed into the harbor in 1792. The First Nations Northwest Coast Salish people were the original residents. Vancouver charted the area of what is now Burrard Inlet. The bay and the city were named in his honor. In 1827, a Hudson Bay Trading camp was set up along the banks of the Fraser River. In 1858, gold was discovered. The first area to develop in 1867 is what is now called Gastown, so named for Gassy Jack Deighton. It's said that Gassy Jack, not happy that the mill, the only building in Burrard Inlet, didn't allow drinking, so he challenged the workers to build him a saloon where he'd sell them whiskey. The saloon was built in a day and Gastown was born. This downtown neighborhood of historic brownstones and warehouses is popular with locals and visitors. There is an eclectic array of shops and restaurants and striking architecture like the Hotel Europe. Every summer Gastown hosts an internationally acclaimed jazz festival. The old steam clock – said to be the only of its kind - is a reminder of Vancouver's Victorian past. From the cruise terminal Gastown is an easy five minute walk down Water Street.

Next door is Chinatown. With its pagoda - shaped telephone booths and its outdoor food stalls, Chinatown is one of the most vibrant neighborhoods of the city. From here, it is just a few blocks to Vancouver's downtown and commercial district. To get a look at modern Vancouver, take the elevator up the observation area of Harbor Center where you get a panoramic 360° view from 500 feet up. At the observation level, helpful guides will answer any questions you may have about the city, including ones about what to see and do.

The hub of downtown is Robson Square. In the square you'll find vendors and street performers as well as the Vancouver Art Gallery. During the summer the steps are a favorite spot for lunch on a sunny day. The museum or "gallery" is worth a visit; don't miss the Emily Carr exhibit on the fourth floor. Her work truly captures the spirit of the Northwest. Shoppers won't want to miss a stroll down Robson Street or a stop at the indoor Pacific Centre mall. Across from the Fairmont Hotel with its green copper roof is the Christ Church Cathedral, which features beautiful stained glass windows and is open to the public

Have an afternoon free? Then you won't want to miss the University of British Columbia and its fantastic Museum of Anthropology. Perched on the cliffs of Point Grey, the museum has one of the most comprehensive collections of Northwest Coast First Nation's art. There is hall after hall of totem poles, house boards, potlatch bowls, masks and weavings representing the Kwakwaka'wakw (Kwakuitl), Nisga'a, Gitxsan, Haida, and Coast Salish people. Slide open a drawer and discover precious artifacts or walk through the grounds and explore replicas of Haida clan houses. Don't miss the exhibit of work by world renowned Haida artist Bill Reid. The museum is open daily 10 am – 5 pm during the summer with extended hours (10 am – 9 pm) on Tuesdays. The museum shop features an excellent collection of art, jewelry and books. If you are exploring on your own take the #4, #10, #25, #41, #42, #49 or #99 bus to the UBC campus; the museum is a ten minutes walk from the UBC bus loop.

A highlight is Stanley Park, second largest urban park in North America after New York City's Central Park. Stanley Park was established in 1889 and contains 1,000 acres of wooded land with an aquarium, lighthouse, rose garden, open air theater, pitch 'n putt, tennis courts, miniature railway, children's farmyard, horse drawn carriage tours, 8 km sea wall, totem park and cricket field. From the cruise terminal it is about a 30 minute walk, or you can hop on the #19 Stanley Park bus on Pender Street and Granville. At the north end of Stanley Park, the majestic Lions Gate Bridge, named for the Lion's Gate peaks, stretches to North Vancouver. The bridge is 1500 feet wide from support to support, and 200 feet high from waterline to mid-span. The Lions Gate Peaks, which can be seen from Vancouver, were so named because they look like the crouching lions in front of the British Museum.

> The iridescent yellow piles of substance to the north east of the bridge are sulfur. Transported from Alberta, it is shipped by rail to Vancouver where it is loaded on ships for distribution around the Pacific Rim.
>
> **FACTS**

The farmer's market at Granville Island is fun to explore; bring your appetite, as there are plenty of places for a great meal. For more information on what to see and do during your stay in Vancouver, visit the Visitor Centre, conveniently located across from the Canada Place cruise terminal, on the plaza level at 200 Burrard Street.

VICTORIA

Coordinates: 48° 25' N, 123° 22' W

Population (2008):   Greater Victoria - 330,000

Called the Cultural Capital of Canada, Victoria, the provincial capital of British Columbia, is one of the most beautiful and livable cities in the world. From the horse-drawn buggies that trot through town to the stately elegance of high tea at The Empress Hotel, Victoria is a slice of the best of Olde England on the west coast of Canada. *Conde Nast Traveler* voted Victoria one of the world's best cities – can't beat that.

Located at the southern tip of Vancouver Island, the city is sheltered from the wind and rain off the Straits of Juan de Fuca, allowing the capital to bask in warmer temperatures and sunnier days than nearby Vancouver. The area was the traditional homeland of the Lekammen people, members of the Northwest Coast Salish culture. There were ten Lekammen villages where the present city now stands. In 1842, James Douglas scouted the area for the Hudson Bay Company and established Fort Victoria in 1843. It was named for Queen Victoria in 1852, and served as the parliamentary capital of Crown Colonies of Vancouver Island since 1856. A highlight of a visit to Victoria includes a visit to the Parliament building, which was completed in 1897.

Across the street from the Parliament building is the world famous Empress Hotel, which no visitor to Victoria can leave without admiring. High tea is still served; reservations are requested. Considered to be one of the best museums in the world, the Royal British Columbia Museum is within walking distance from both Parliament and The Empress. Started in 1886, the museum contains the best collection of Northwest Coast art you will

ever see. There is also a fascinating recreation of life in early Victoria. Not far away on picture-perfect Victoria Harbor is the Maritime Museum of British Columbia. Don't care much for history? The city is a mecca for ethnic dining and great shopping, especially if your interests are in items exported from the United Kingdom. Eaton Centre is the city's downtown mall. Though the city has grown in recent years it still retains its quaint provincial charm.

For many, Victoria is synonymous with world famous Butchart Gardens. Once the site of a huge cement quarry, the 55 acre garden contains 1,000,000 bedding plants each season! Visitors are dazzled by the splendor of the gardens that can be enjoyed both day and night.

CAMPBELL RIVER

Coordinates: 49° 58′ N, 125° 13′ W
Population (2009):   31,294

South of Seymour Narrows and Quadra Island, Campbell River stretches fifteen miles down the east coast of Vancouver Island. The smoke stack of the city's pulp mill dominates the skyline. For those lucky enough to explore the city, it is a beautiful getaway filled with wonderful outdoor recreational possibilities. The Campbell River Museum has an excellent collection of Northwest Coast artifacts including a beautiful display of dance masks. From Campbell River visitors can take whale-watching trips or even spot a killer whale or two from the Rotary Sidewalk or Discovery Fishing Pier. Fisherman may want to try their hand at becoming a member of the world-famous Tyee Club. Members must use a simple, non-motorized row boat to catch a Tyee (or King) salmon of 30 pounds or more! Strathcona Provincial Park is a wonderland for hikers and Campbell River is also the gateway to the Golden Hinde (7,218 feet), tallest peak on Vancouver Island.

ALERT BAY/CORMORANT ISLAND

Coordinates: 50° 35′ N, 126° 55′ W
Population (2006):   556

North of Vancouver Island and southeast of Malcolm Island, Cormorant Island is the home of the First Nations Community of Alert Bay. This "Kwakuitl" or Kwakwaka'wakw community is known for its rich history of traditional arts and carving. During the era of the Indian Act (which in

1876 prohibited the potlatch, totem pole carving and practicing of other traditional ways) many communities lost much of their culture. Not Alert Bay. The community continued to act in defiance of the law, taking the penalty of fines and incarceration. In 1921, 45 people from the community were charged with holding a potlatch. Huge rooms in the Royal BC Museum in Victoria are dedicated to the goods confiscated during potlatch raids as well as the newspaper articles that followed. When the Act was repealed in 1951, Alert Bay had not lost touch with its traditions. Other Kwakuitl communities turned to Alert Bay to learn from its elders and carvers. Today some of the most famous carvers in the province come from Alert Bay.

FACTS

Alert Bay is home to the world's tallest totem pole. The pole is 173 feet tall and it is made of two parts measuring 168 feet and 5 feet. It was carved by chief carver Jimmy Dick in 1972. From a distance it looks like a skinny stick but look carefully and you can see that it depicts the various tribes of the community. The pole is carved but you will need very good binoculars to see the detail from the ship!

Other examples of fine carving can be seen in the town. As you face the bay, look to the right and you will see what looks like a cinder block retaining wall and a green, park-like area. This is the old Kwakuitl cemetery; many of these poles are mortuary or memorial poles. With binoculars you can see the intricate feathering techniques used by the Alert Bay carvers to represent the family crests.

Also at the far end of the bay are two buildings constructed in the traditional clan house style with iconographic renderings of totemic figures. One of the buildings is the U'mista Cultural Centre which has one of the finest collections of potlatch masks, ceremonial regalia, and coppers in the world. Many of these items were confiscated by the government during the Indian Act and have been repatriated in response to a community mandate. Behind the U'mista Cultural Centre is the Namgis Big House. At the base of the world's tallest pole is the Namgis Big House. Built in 1963, it resembles a traditional Kwakuitl long house or "big" house. The original building burned in 1997 but was rebuilt in 1999.

In the 1970's, to qualify for government monies, many people in Alert Bay applied for small business loans. To constitute a business, private vehicles were converted into taxis. Consequently, Alert Bay holds the world's record for having the most number of taxis per mile of road anywhere – 11 taxis per two miles of road!

The partially-abandoned brick building is what remains of St. Michael's Residential School. Built in 1929, its purpose was to remove Kwakuitl children from neighboring villages and acculturate them in Western ways while providing a basic education and vocational skills including carpentry, boat building and fishing. Children were instructed in English and prohibited from speaking their own language or playing native games. The school ceased classes in 1975. In a historic move on June 11, 2008, Canadian Prime Minister Stephen Harper apologized to all Native people affected by over one hundred years of residential school abuse, admitting, "Children should never have been taken from their loving homes or vibrant culture." The building was turned over to the Namgis community in 1973 and now contains offices of the tribal council.

Alert Bay has a resident bugler! If your ship slows down to view the community he may come out and play a few tunes. He usually greets ships with a rendition of, "Oh, Canada," and "The Star Spangled Banner."

TERRY'S TIPS

BELLA BELLA

Coordinates: 52° 09′ N, 128° 10′ W

Population (2006):   1127

Located between Lama Passage and Milbanke Sound, Campbell Island is the home of the First Nations Community of Bella Bella. The original community of Bella Bella was across Lama Passage on Denny Island. The Hudson Bay Trading Company established Ft. McLoughlin, which soon became very prosperous. When the population grew too big for Denny Island, the community moved across to Campbell Island. After Ft. McLoughlin closed, the people of Bella Bella were ready to go back to their traditional ways-- but things had changed. The Indian Act prohibited all First Nations people in coastal British Columbia from holding a pot-latch, carving totems, or speaking their own language. Children were sent far away to Indian Schools and the community morale had deteriorated. No one wanted to stay. In 1951, when the Indian Act was finally repealed many people had forgotten their culture. By the 1970's unemployment was 90%. Councilman Cecil Reid asked the provincial government for $30 million in loans to infuse the community with industry and infrastructure. Today the town has a growing population, new housing, ferry dock and airport, cable TV station, and a new Native cultural center. Unemployment has dropped to 12%.

PRINCE RUPERT

Coordinates: 54° 19′ N, 130° 18′ W

Population (2009):   15,281

The natural harbor of what now is Prince Rupert was favored for centuries by the First Nations Haida people of the Northwest Coast. Today it is recognized as the 3rd largest ice-free harbor in the world. In the 1870's, settlers came to establish fishing camps and canneries. Today the oldest surviving cannery in British Columbia is in Prince Rupert. However, in 1910, Charles Melville Hays took a good look at Prince Rupert and felt it was the perfect location from which to hub Canada's west coast trans-portation system. It was Hays who noted that Prince Rupert was closer to Japan than Vancouver. He saw the development of a great harbor that would link with the western terminus of a then-proposed transcontinen-tal rail line. He was so inspired; he went to England to raise money for his project. Returning back to Canada in 1912, he made the unfortunate choice of booking passage across the Atlantic on the HMS Titanic! The

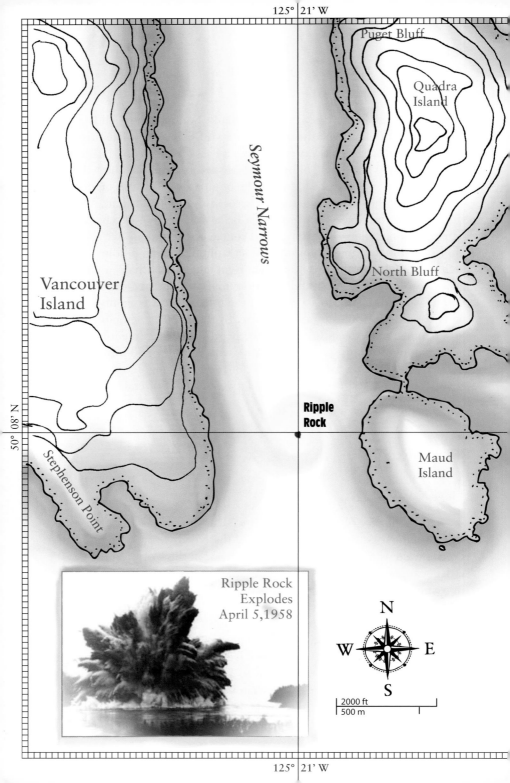

125° 21' W

Puget Bluff

Quadra
Island

Seymour Narrows

North Bluff

Vancouver
Island

**Ripple
Rock**

Stephenson Point

Maud
Island

50° 08' N

Ripple Rock
Explodes
April 5, 1958

N

W   E

S

2000 ft
500 m

125° 21' W

town, located in northern coastal British Columbia, was formally incorporated in 1910 and named after the son of Queen Elizabeth and Frederick of Bohemia. In addition to the Alaska Marine Highway ferries that call upon the port, many cruise ships now visit Prince Rupert. Passengers are delighted with the area around the docks where old warehouses are now converted to shops. Prince Rupert has the feel of a real town on the Canadian frontier.

SCENIC SAILING

SEYMOUR NARROWS
Coordinates: 50° 08' N, 125° 21' W

Located between Quadra Island and Vancouver Island, Seymour Narrows at ½ mile in width is the most narrow portion of Discovery Passage and is also the most narrow passage of your cruise. Your transit through Seymour Narrows is exciting, scenic and historic. Your ship will be navigating through some of the most difficult waters for commercial traffic anywhere in the world. Though the Narrows are only 1½ miles long, prior to 1958, it was 1½ miles of pure dread.

Large vessels sailing up the coast of British Columbia have only two choices: travel via the rough seas of the open Pacific or via the calm waters between Vancouver Island and the mainland. Unfortunately, no other passage is deep enough for the draft of large ships except Seymour Narrows. One thousand foot cliffs hem in the rushing water, causing currents in the constricted Narrows to run at 15 knots (16.5 mph!) Whirlpools and eddies can capsize a small boat. Prior to 1958, one boat a year was destroyed in Seymour Narrows, which was first charted in 1792 by Captain George Vancouver. By 1875, 117 people had lost their lives in navigationally related accidents. To make things worse -- there was a huge rock hidden only 9 feet beneath the sea in the middle of the narrowest point – Ripple Rock. Something needed to be done.

In 1943, the first attempt was made to blast away Ripple Rock. A barge was held in place, attached to Ripple Rock by 250-ton anchors and cables. Within 24 hours the first cable snapped from the vibration of the constant current and the project was abandoned. In 1945, bolts were drilled in the shore to anchor the barge but were sheared off from the strain. In 1955, 75 men started to dig 6 feet of tunneling a day. In three years 3,600 ft. of

vertical and horizontal underwater tunnels were dug from Maude Island to Ripple Rock. In total 1,375 tons of dynamite were loaded, and on April 5, 1958, the largest, deliberately set, non-nuclear blast to date was exploded in Seymour Narrows, finally destroying Ripple Rock!

Though Ripple Rock is gone, ships can only transit Seymour Narrows during slack water – in between high and low tides. Therefore your captain has a narrow window of time to go through. If delays cause the ship to miss its window, it must wait 6 hours for the next slack water-- just another reminder that Mother Nature is still in control.

LANDMARKS AND POINTS OF INTEREST

ARISTAZABAL ISLAND
Coordinates: 52° 38′ N, 129° 05′ W

Island located east of Hecate Strait, west of Laredo Channel

ASHDOWN ISLAND
Coordinates: 53° 04′ N, 129° 14′ W

Small island located south of Gil Island; time permitting your ship may slow down to pass the rock, which is a favorite for sea lions.

BOAT BLUFF LIGHTHOUSE

Coordinates: 52° 46′ N, 128° 30′ W

Located on the southwest tip of Sarah Island, the charming lighthouse at Boat Bluff is still manpowered. Two families live as the resident lighthouse keepers. Notice the signature red roofs of the Canadian lighthouses. If the ship sounds its horns, no doubt you will see one of the family members and a few dogs coming out for a wave!

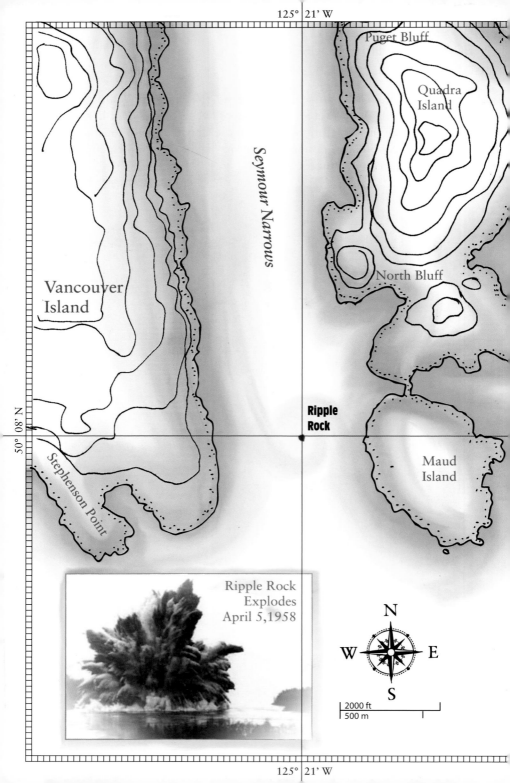

125° 21' W

Puget Bluff

Quadra
Island

Seymour Narrows

North Bluff

Vancouver
Island

**Ripple
Rock**

Stephenson Point

Maud
Island

50° 08' N

Ripple Rock
Explodes
April 5, 1958

N

W   E

S

2000 ft
500 m

125° 21' W

BUTEDALE

Coordinates: 53° 09' N - 128° 42' W

Located on the east side of Princess Royal Island, Butedale was once a thriving cannery that employed over 300 people. Started in the 1930's by the Canadian Fish Canning Company, the cannery closed in the early 1970's. The buildings now abandoned are privately owned. A few people live on-site and run a bait shop with hot showers. Fishermen know beautiful Butedale Falls for its trout.

CAMPANIA ISLAND

Coordinates: 53° 05' N, 129° 25' W

Island located west of Squally Channel and east of the Esteven Islands.

DENNY ISLAND

Coordinates: 52° 07' N, 128° 04' W

Located between Lama Passage and Fisher Channel, Denny Island was the original home of the native community of Bella Bella. Between 1833 – 1899, the Kwakuitl village of Old Bella Bella co-existed with the Hudson Bay Trading operation at Ft. McLoughlin. Soon the original town site became too small and the community moved across Lama Passage to its present site.

DRYAD POINT LIGHTHOUSE

Coordinates: 52° 18' N, 128° 11' W

Located on Campbell Island, it is one of the distinctive lighthouses of coastal B.C.

FARRANT ISLAND

Coordinates: 53° 21' N, 129° 23' W

Island located to the west of Grenville Channel at the southern entrance

FINLAYSON CHANNEL

Coordinates: 52° 34' 60 N, 128° 28' W

Located between Princess Royal Island and the provincial mainland north of the Boat Bluff Lighthouse, this channel has a depth of 2,400 ft.

GIL ISLAND

Coordinates: 53° 12' N, 129° 14' W

Island located northeast of Campania Island and northwest of Princess Royal Island. See Ashdown Island on page 126.

GRENVILLE CHANNEL

Coordinates: 53° 37' N, 129° 43' W

This picturesque 47 mile long channel was carved out thousands of years ago by ancient glaciers. The deep narrow waterway marks the channel as a fjord. Portions of the channel are over 300 feet deep. Grenville Channel was named for William Wyndham Grenville, (1759-1834) who was Prime Minister of England from 1806 – 1807. The steep mountainsides close in at Tom Island. Ormiston Point is the narrowest part of the channel measuring less than 1/4 mile wide.

HADDINGTON ISLAND

Coordinates: 50° 36′ N, 127° 01′ W

Almost perfectly circular, Haddington Island is located north of Cormorant Island, west of Malcolm Island and east of Port McNeil on Vancouver Island. In addition to its shape, Haddington Island is famous for being the site from which granite was quarried and used in the construction of the Parliament building in Victoria.

HECATE STRAIT

Coordinates: 52° 23′ N, 130° 12′ W (southern entrance)

Body of water north of Queen Charlotte Sound and south of Dixon Entrance, east of Queen Charlotte Islands.

JOHNSTONE STRAIT

Coordinates: 50° 31′ N, 126° 39′ W

Body of water approximately 64 miles long running parallel to Vancouver Island's east coast from Telegraph Cove to Rock Bay. The concentration of currents from the surrounding islands brings in lots of fish, making this prime killer whale territory. Robson Bight is a cove on eastern Vancouver Island along Johnstone Strait.

LAREDO CHANNEL

Coordinates: 52° 44′ N, 129° 05′ W

Waterway east of Aristazabal Island and west of Princess Royal Island. Popular channel used by many cruise ships and the occasional humpback whale.

LAMA PASSAGE

Coordinates: 52° 05′ N, 128° 07′ W

Sixteen mile long passage between Campbell and Denny Islands. Narrows to 800 feet between Saunders and Campbell Islands at Dryad Point.

MAUDE ISLAND

Coordinates: 50° 11 N, 125° 20 W

Small island located at the southern entrance to Seymour Narrows; used to anchor machinery during attempts to blast Ripple Rock.

MONTOCK ISLAND

Coordinates: 52° 37′ N, 128° 30′ W

Located east of Swindle Island and southwest of Sarah Island, this conical island has been called "Cone Island" or "China Hat" for its distinctive shape.

MT. BAKER, WASHINGTON STATE

Elevation: 10,778 feet
Coordinates: 48° 46′ N, 121° 48′ W

Mt. Baker, like Mt. Rainier, is a dormant volcano.

MT. RAINIER

Elevation: 14,411 feet
Coordinates: 46° 51′ N, 121° 45′ W

Tallest peak of the Cascade Mountain range and tallest peak in Washington State, Mt. Rainier is a dormant volcano. It contains the most extensive system of glaciers outside of Alaska. Named in 1792, by Captain George Vancouver for his friend Rear Admiral Peter Rainier, it was originally called "Tacoma" or "Tahoma" – snowy one – by the Native residents.

PITT ISLAND

Coordinates: 53° 30'N, 129° 49 W

Located to the west of Grenville Channel, the island was named for William Pitt (1759-1806) who was Prime Minister of England from 1783 – 1801 and 1804-1806. Pitt sailed under George Vancouver.

PORT HARDY

Coordinates: 50° 43' N, 127° 30' W

Located on Vancouver Island, Port Hardy is the northernmost community on the eastern side of the island.

PORT MCNEIL

Coordinates: 50° 35' N, 127° 05' W

Located on the east side of north Vancouver Island, Port McNeil is south of Malcolm Island.

PRINCESS ROYAL CHANNEL

Coordinates: 53° 10' N, 128° 40' W

Waterway between Princess Royal Island and Coast Mountains on the mainland.

PRINCESS ROYAL ISLAND

Coordinates: 52° 55' N, 128° 50' W

Large island located east of Aristazabal Island and north of Swindle Island. Named for the fur trading vessel, Princess Royal, it was commanded by Charles Duncan who named his ship for Charlotte Augusta Matilda (1788-1828), 1st daughter and 4th child of King George III and Queen Charlotte. Back in the 1890's the island was bustling; first with logging camps then gold mines. The town of Surf (pop. 350) had a hydroelectric facility, school, hospital and even a movie theater. In the 1930's it was declared the highest producing hard rock gold mine in British Columbia. However, like so many towns of the era, nothing remains today but the stories.

PUGET SOUND

Coordinates: 47° 29′ N, 122° 25′ W

Named by Captain George Vancouver in 1792 for Lieutenant Peter Puget, the 83 mile sound is really a fjord carved out by ancient glaciation. Like most fjords it is extremely deep and dark, making it the perfect home of the giant Pacific octopus, the world's largest known octopus variety. Lt. Puget was ordered to survey the area and was sent off in a launch and cutter with Joseph Whidbey, for whom Whidbey Island was named.

PULTENEY POINT LIGHTHOUSE

Coordinates: 51° 10′ N, 127° 46′ W

Located at the north entrance of Queen Charlotte Strait between Vancouver Island and the mainland. Lighthouse was built in 1907 and rebuilt in 1945.

QUADRA ISLAND

Coordinates: 50° 11′ N, 125° 18′ W

Large island located to the east of Vancouver Island at Seymour Narrows.

QUEEN CHARLOTTE ISLANDS (HAIDA GWAII)

Coordinates: 53° 55′ N, 132° 24′ W

Also known as Haida Gwaii, the archipelago is located north of Vancouver Island. First spotted by Spanish explorer Juan Perez in 1774 and later Captain James Cook in 1778, the islands were surveyed and named in 1787 by Captain Charles Dixon, who named them for the wife of King George III. In 2009 the islands returned to their original First Nations name.

QUEEN CHARLOTTE SOUND

Coordinates: 51° 48′ N, 129° 38′ W

Body of water south of Queen Charlotte Islands.

ROBSON BIGHT

Coordinates: 50° 27′ N, 126° 17′ W

Small cove on Vancouver Island located south of Johnstone Strait, the shallow waters and smooth stones of Robson Bight make it a favorite spot for killer whales to come and rub their stomachs against the rocks. Throughout the year but especially during late summer when the salmon run chances are good, you may spot killer whales here or close by. Due to the fragile nature of the cove it is designated a Protected Ecological Area and ships cannot approach too closely.

SARAH ISLAND

Coordinates: 52° 46′ N, 128° 30′ W

Located between Finlayson Channel and Sarah Passage east of Princess Royal Island.

SOINTULA/MALCOLM ISLAND

Coordinates: 50° 38′ N, 127° 01′ W

Approximately 15 miles in length east to west, Malcolm Island is located southwest of Queen Charlotte Strait, north of Vancouver Island. The main town is Sointula. Founded in the 1901, Sointula was a utopian agrarian community started by a group of Finnish immigrants headed by Matti Kurikka of the Kalevan Kansa Colonization Company. Though Sointula means "harmony," the community never realized its idealistic goals, and the Colonization Company ended in 1905. However, many descendants of the original community remain, making Sointula a vibrant town with traditional Finnish roots. It published Canada's first Finnish-language newspaper, Aika, from 1901-1905.

STRAIT OF GEORGIA

Coordinates: 49° 14′ N, 123° 36′ W (south)

Body of water that begins in the south at Haro Strait north of the Strait of Juan de Fuca and continues north to Quadra Island, paralleling Vancouver Island and forming the first portion of British Columbia's Inside Passage.

STRAIT OF JUAN DE FUCA

Coordinates: 48° 14′ N, 123° 11′ W

This 90 mile long waterway is the northwestern most international boundary between the United States and Canada. It extends between Vancouver Island and the Olympic Peninsula. The strait was named in 1592 by a Greek sailing master Apostolos Valerieanos, who called himself Juan de Fuca. Early Spanish charts used by the British contain this name, giving credence to the fact he indeed did first chart the area.

SWINDLE ISLAND

Coordinates: 52° 33′ N, 128° 25′ W

Located south of Princess Royal Island and north of Price Island.

TOLMIE CHANNEL

Coordinates: 53° 00′ N, 128° 34′ W

Waterway between Princess Royal Island to the west and the Coast Mountains to the east.

VANCOUVER ISLAND

Coordinates: 49° 17′ N, 123° 07′ W

The 11th largest island in Canada, Vancouver Island is 280 miles long and is one of the few geographical features that can be seen from space. Named for Captain George Vancouver, the 12,355-square-mile island is home to the provincial capital of Victoria, located at its southern tip.

WORK ISLAND

Coordinates: 53° 10′ N, 128° 40′ W

A small island between the mainland and Princess Royal Island in Princess Royal Channel, it is directly north of the Butedale Cannery.

CITIES AND TOWNS

KETCHIKAN

Coordinates:	55° 20' N, 131° 38' W
Population (2010):	12,984

Ketchikan means Eagle Wing River in Tlingit. The Tlingit knew that the streams surrounding their village were teeming with salmon, and where there are salmon there are eagles. Later when the white men came, they too capitalized on the abundance of salmon, founding in 1897 a cannery, where the present town now stands. Like most towns in Southeast Alaska, Ketchikan – Alaska's fourth largest city - is on an island, Revillagigedo Island, which is known as "Revilla" for short. Located at the southernmost extent of the Tongass National Forest, timber, fishing and mining has been the mainstay of the community since its incorporation in 1900. Many of the buildings along Front Street still retain a turn-of-the-century feel. One of the most historic and colorful areas is Creek Street. Located on Salmon Creek, the stilted houses were used as bordellos during canning days. The local joke is Ketchikan was the only place where both men and salmon went upstream to spawn. Today the area has been renovated and contains many shops for the visitor along its boardwalk. Just behind Creek Street is the funicular up to the Cape Fox Lodge Hotel; from the hotel you will have a great view of Ketchikan. If you are up for a walk you can return back to town via either the trail down to the fish hatchery and the Totem Heritage Center, or Married Man's Trail (so named for the obvious.)

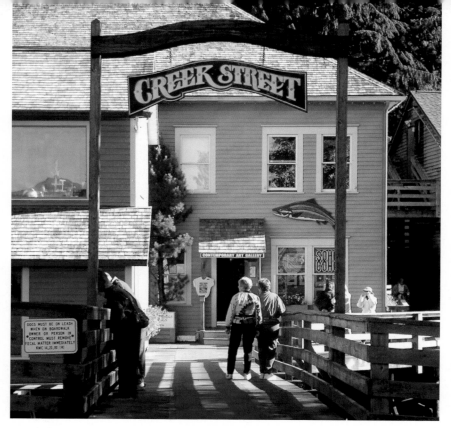

Ketchikan is known by several monikers: Rain Capital of the United States (162 inches average), Salmon Capital, Gateway City as well as First City (first city along the panhandle heading north), and Native American Capital of the state. Ketchikan has the largest population of Native Ameri-

Ketchikan Jokes

Did you hear the one about the traveling salesman? A salesman was sent to Ketchikan for three days. Each day was worse than the last with rain, rain and more rain. Finally on the third day, the salesman put on his raincoat and galoshes then grabbed his umbrella, and was standing on the street corner waiting for the light to change when a little boy walked up and stood next to him. 'Son,' the man said, 'do you have any idea how long it's been raining?' The little boy looked up at the man and said, 'gee no, mister, I'm only seven years old."

cans on a per capita basis, more than any other city in the state, and the Northwest Coast influence is strongly felt throughout the community. The Northwest Coast Native Americans of Ketchikan include not just Tlingit but also Haida and Tsimshian. In addition to the shops and galleries featuring Native art, enjoy the Totem Heritage Center which contains the oldest totem poles in the state; Totem Bight State Park for the largest collection of totem poles (many of them authentic reproductions); and Saxman Village, a working Tlingit community with some of the most interesting totem poles in the state. Throughout Ketchikan totem poles have been carved and raised, telling the story of individuals as well as myths and legends in Tlingit culture. Take a moment to read the interpretive signs. Two famous totem poles are along Creek Street next to the library, which is also the home of Ketchikan's small city museum.

Across Tongass Narrows is Pennock Island; the island has been a quiet spot for weekend fishing cabins or second homes. Bounded by the Tongass National Forest to the east and the Tongass Narrow to the west, the borough of Ketchikan has a limited amount of space in which to grow. Consequently, more and more people are moving out to Pennock Island, prompting speculation that a bridge may one day be built from Revilla Island to Pennock and on to Gravina Island. That speculative bridge became known as the, "Bridge to Nowhere" made famous during the 2008 presidential campaign. There is not much on Gravina Island except the Ketchikan International Airport; and yes, it is an international airport, as there are flights to Canada. Because there is no bridge between the islands passengers must take a small ferry across the Tongass Narrows to catch a plane. As you pass the airport notice the pier used for float planes; this is the airport's connecting terminal, Ketchikan-style.

> The Ketchikan International Airport has the claim to fame of being the only airport in the world where the runway is higher than the control tower.

FACTS

Directly behind the city is Deer Mountain at 3001 feet. Locals consider it the most accurate source of weather prediction. If you can't see the top of Deer Mountain – it's raining; if you can – it's going to rain! Dress for the weather and enjoy Ketchikan.

Local Treats

Everyone who is anyone knows about Ketchi Candies. This locally owned and operated candy shop on 315 Mission Street, has been satisfying the cravings of locals and visitors since 1993. Stop in to sample one of their specialty flavors of fudge. Do not leave without purchasing at least one box of their world-famous chocolate-covered Oreos. Long before anyone else, the folks at Ketchi Candies were dippin' cookies. You will not be disappointed. PS: Whenever I want to give a special gift from Alaska, my first choice is a box of Ketchi Candies – no one ever complains!

WRANGELL

Coordinates:	56° 28′ N, 132° 22′ W
Population (2009):	1,990

Wrangell is the last deep water port in Southeast Alaska to be developed for tourism. It still retains much of its original Alaskan character, something lost by other more commercial ports. Some fun facts about Wrangell: John Muir made Wrangell his base during his exploration of Southeast Alaska; Sheriff Wyatt Earp was deputy Marshall for ten days. Located on Wrangell Island, the town is in a beautiful setting. Like most of Southeast, Wrangell's economy was tied to fishing and lumber; however, with the close of its mill, many residents started to reassess the community's desirability as a cruise destination.

In the "good ol' days," Boy Scouts selling garnets in tin muffin trays and costumed ladies greeted visitors on the pier. Most people came in on the ferry. Few cruise ships called upon the port. Little by little that is changing, and the town is responding.

From the pier, there are several options of exploration on foot. Turn to your left, along the beach, and you will see over forty ancient petroglyphs, the largest collection of rock art in Southeast Alaska. These inscriptions in stone were left by the ancestors of today's Native community. No one is sure if the renderings are Tlingit, Haida, Tsimshian, or maybe even groups crossing to the coast from the interior. The petroglyphs, which archaeologists date back to 8,000 years, are protected as part of the Petroglyph State Historic Park. Sanctioned rubbings are available for purchase in town.

From your ship you can see the beautiful new Wrangell Museum. The museum houses an excellent, eclectic collection of artifacts as well as priceless archaeological findings from the Prince of Wales Island dig. It has the oldest known Tlingit house posts. Wrangell's Russian and Gold

TIPS

For golfers who want to say they have played it all, Wrangell has a golf course - 9 hole Muskeg Meadows. Located along the forest edge, there is no other course like it in the world. If the ground is too wet you can tee off on a piece of astro-turf. But the best part of the The Meadows is the handicap – the raven handicap – when and if a raven steals your ball - which they do!

Rush history is also represented in photographs and artifacts. Previously the museum was housed in an old building in town. However, through the generous endowment by Dr. James and Mrs. Elsie Nolan, the museum was made possible.

Also of historical and cultural interest is Kik-setti Totem Park and Chief Shakes Island. Visible from the museum, this was the original site of the Chief Shakes Tribal House. In 1939, the house was restored and made a National Historical Monument. The tribal house contains excellent examples of Tlingit carving and iconography.

Wrangell is the gateway to the Stikine - Le Conte Wilderness. Jet boats will whisk you across Stikine Strait where wildlife is often seen on shore. Trips are also available to the LeConte Glacier. The Boy Scout camp from which the famous garnets are collected is nearby, on Garnet Mountain.

If you want to get close to nature without taking a tour try Rainbow Falls; just follow the boardwalk and you'll pass through beautiful old growth forest on your way to this impressive waterfall.

131° 07' W

N
W E
S

MISTY FJORDS
NATIONAL MONUMENT

10 mi
20 km

Burrough's Bay

Chickamin River

Behm Canal

Walker Cove

Rudyerd Bay

The Punchbowl

Revillagigedo
Island

55° 30' N

NEW EDDYSTONE ROCK P. 151

Winstanley
Island

Smeaton
Island

Smeaton Bay

Ketchikan

Annette
Island

Mary
Island

*Mary Island
Lighthouse*

Cat
Island

Boca de Quadra

131° 07' W

SCENIC SAILING

MISTY FJORDS

Coordinates: 55° 32′ N, 130° 51′ W

At the southern tip of the maze of islands that form Alaska's panhandle lies Misty Fjords National Monument. Accessible only by air or sea, it is pristine wilderness located east of Revillagigedo Island. Float planes from Ketchikan, 22 miles away, tour the area and are permitted to land in designated mountain lakes and inlets. Flights can be booked through your tour desk onboard. However, since the other option for visiting this wilderness is by sea, many excursion boats call on Misty Fjords, as do a few cruise ships.

Misty Fjords became a National Monument in 1978; with 2.3 million acres of land it is the second largest protected wilderness area in the country. It is located amidst the 17 million acre Tongass National Forest, largest national forest in the country. Tongass was one of the first national forests to be set aside for protection and preservation against the ravages of industry. Theodore Roosevelt created Tongass National Forest in 1908. Today 80% of the forest is protected from timber harvesting.

The name says it all; Misty Fjords is a spectacularly beautiful misty fjord. Three-thousand foot granite cliffs rise straight up out of the sea, their tops shrouded in ethereal fingers of mist. In the early morning, low wispy clouds comb their way through stands of Sitka spruce and red cedar trees. Eagles perch on trees along the shore and look so close you could reach out and touch them. Due to the ideal conditions between land and sea few areas contain as many species of unusual animals. Within the temperate rainforest you are likely to see mountain goat, brown bear, black bear, moose, and river otter. The sea is filled with all five species of Pacific salmon. Spawning salmon attract bear as well as killer whale. The salmon must share their rivers and streams with Dolly Varden char, cutthroat trout, steelhead, and grayling. Steller sea lions and harbor seals also make their home in Misty Fjords.

By definition a fjord is a glacially carved valley that has been filled in by the sea. Misty Fjords is no exception. Not too long ago in geologic time the land was covered by 4,000 feet of ice. Most of this area of Southeast Alaska is now free of glacial ice; the northeastern corner of the national monument, however, still contains an area of active glaciers. As the ice retreated, the sea filled in these steep narrow "U" shaped valleys and bowls.

The Punchbowl, with its 3,000 foot granite cliffs, is a magnificent example of a glacially carved bowl.

Your approach to Misty Fjords will be by way of the Behm Canal. Though the national monument is made up of many navigable fjords, Rudyerd Bay is probably the most scenic. About 45 minutes prior to your arrival at the mouth of Rudyerd Bay, your ship will pass New Eddystone Rock. This 200-foot-high tower of rock is a volcanic plug or what is left of a volcanic vent. The Coast Mountains were created by the uplifting of the North American plate. At this collision point friction is created, producing earthquakes and volcanoes all around the Pacific Rim. The flanks of the ancient plug have long eroded away, leaving this unusual formation of basalt in the middle of the canal.

Cruising through Rudyerd Bay is magical. The protected inlet is so calm it mirrors the image of the mountains and the trees. Ribbons of water glisten down the cliffs from beneath the low lying mist. From the bay's entrance, on the starboard side at Mile 2.5 is the Punchbowl. The inlet is a little over 2 miles long with an incredible depth of 900 feet. Known for its 3,000 foot granite cliffs, the Punchbowl is a favorite spot for mountain goats and rock climbers.

Mile 9 is where Rudyerd Bay branches off, forming a "T" to the north and south. The branch to the south is not as deep as the branch to the north, so most ships continue to the north, which is the port side. Besides the technical reason, another reason for making this choice is that the northern branch of the bay contains two salmon creeks that are favorites with the local bears. If your ship sails up the north branch, the first bear creek at Mile 10 will be located on the starboard side, the second bear creek will be on the port side. Look for the break in the trees which is where the stream widens out into a broad wash. Bears may be seen up the creek bed as well as along the beach. Black bears seem to prefer the first creek while brown bears are more often seen at creek two.

By mid-morning float planes from Ketchikan start their flightseeing. After you've spent hours selfishly enjoying the silence of the wilderness, the planes seem like huge mechanical mosquitoes and are just about as annoying. But, admittedly, they provide an excellent service; and are the only other alternative for many to visit this remarkably beautiful natural area. During a flightseeing program planes do have permission to land and many stop on alpine lakes where guests can walk out onto the pontoons and enjoy the silence.

Throughout most of the summer but especially during the beginning of the season, you may notice what looks like fluorescent green patches of pollution floating from the bay. Fear not. It is NOT pollution but rather pollen. In the middle of the largest national forest in the United States, pollen bursts out into the air, carried along by wind and rain accumulating in these swirling pools of green. Eventually the pollen will beach and hopefully provide new growth to a new area.

FACTS

SNOW PASSAGE

Coordinates: 56° 16′ N, 132° 57′ W

Snow Passage – also called Snow Pass - is one of those places you want
to make sure to see; its scenic beauty is unsurpassed regardless if you are
sailing through in the morning or the evening. Your ship will pass through
Snow Passage on its way to or from Ketchikan. Not only is it beautiful; it
is a very good place for spotting wildlife. The narrow passage and strong
currents make the area ideal for concentrating small fish which whales,
seals and sea lions feed upon. These marine mammals count on Snow
Passage as prime feeding ground. Check out the buoys that mark the passage – sea lions love buoys. Located west of Zarembo Island and Clarence
Strait, the passage was named after USN Lieut. Commander Albert Snow.

LANDMARKS AND POINTS OF INTEREST

AIRPORT
Coordinates: 55° 21' N, 131° 43' W

The Ketchikan International Airport is located on Gravina Island; small ferries take passengers and cars across Tongass Narrows to catch their flights. The airport is known for having the only runway higher than the control tower!

ANAN CREEK
Coordinates: 56° 11' N, 131° 53' W

Located up Bradfield Canal on land protected by the Tongass National Forest, Anan Creek is one of the best places to view bears in the late summer. You must book an excursion to get to Anan Creek, but it's worth it.

BEHM CANAL
Coordinates: 55° 12' N, 131° 07' W

Located between Revillagigedo Island and the mainland, Behm Canal is the gateway to Misty Fjords National Monument. The canal stretches over 100 miles north to south. It was named in 1793 by Captain George Vancouver for Russian Major Magnus Carp von Behm, who generously offered his hospitality to Captain Charles Clerke, who took Cook's ships the Discovery and Resolution to Kamchatka for repair in 1779. It was from Petropavlosk that Clerke sent news to London of Cook's death. Vancouver met Behm during this visit.

CLARENCE STRAIT
Coordinates: 56° 08' N, 132° 46' W

Running north and south along the eastern shore of Prince of Wales Island, Clarence Strait is 125 miles long and was named in 1793 by Captain George Vancouver for Prince William Henry, Duke of Clarence.

GRAVINA ISLAND
Coordinates: 55° 18′ N, 131° 47′ W

Sixteenth largest island in Southeast
Alaska, Gravina Island is sparsely
inhabited. Located west of Ketchikan, between Tongass Narrows
and Clarence Strait, it is the home of
the Ketchikan International Airport,
known for its unusual runway. Name
was probably first given by Jacinto
Camano for Frederico Gravina, a
Spanish naval officer; and adopted by
Captain George Vancouver.

GUARD ISLAND LIGHT HOUSE
Coordinates: 55° 26′ N, 131° 50′ W

Located at the northern entrance to Tongass Narrows, Guard Island Lighthouse was originally built in 1903 and stood 79 feet above the sea. It was
rebuilt in 1924 and automated in 1969.

LINCOLN ROCK LIGHT HOUSE
Coordinates: 56° 03′ N, 132° 42′ W

On Clarence Strait enroute to or from Snow Passage you will pass Lincoln
Rock Lighthouse. The light house was built 1904, reconstructed in 1931,
and automated in 1969.

MARY ISLAND LIGHTHOUSE
Coordinates: 55° 06′ N, 131° 11′ W

East of Annette Island, 15 miles south of Ketchikan, Mary Island Lighthouse is on the northeast corner of Mary Island in Revillagigedo Channel.
The lighthouse was built in 1903 and stood 67 feet above the sea; in 1931
it was rebuilt in its new Art Deco design, and in 1969 it was automated.

NEW EDDYSTONE ROCK

Coordinates: 55° 30′ N, 131° 07′ W

Located on Behm Canal, New Eddystone Rock is an outcropping of basalt produced as a result of ancient volcanic activity. The stone tower rises 200 feet out of the middle of the fjord. It was named by Captain George Vancouver in 1794, after Eddystone Light House located in the English Channel.

PENNOCK ISLAND

Coordinates: 55° 18′ N, 131° 37′ W

The three mile long island is wedged between Revilla Island and Gravina Island on Tongass Narrows, directly west of the city of Ketchikan. Island was named after Homer Pennock, a prospector for whom the town of Homer was also named.

PRINCE OF WALES ISLAND

Coordinates: 56° 14′ N, 133° 23′ W

Largest island in Southeast Alaska and third largest island in the United States after Kodiak and Hawaii; Prince of Wales is 2,231 square miles. Located west of Revilla Island between Clarence Strait and the Pacific, Prince of Wales was named in 1793 by Captain George Vancouver in honor of George, Prince of Wales, who later became King George IV

REVILLAGIGEDO ISLAND

Coordinates: 55° 41′ N, 131° 22′ W

Fifth largest island in Southeast Alaska, Revillagigedo or "Revilla" Island, as the locals call it, is 1,168 square miles. Behm Canal circles around the island from the east to the north, and Tongass Narrows separates Gravina and tiny Pennock Islands to the west. Though the name is commonly attributed to Captain George Vancouver, it was probably first given in 1792 by Jacinto Camano who named it in honor of Don Juan Vincente de Guemes Pacheco de Padilla Horcasitas, Count of Revilla Gigedo and Viceroy of Mexico.

RUDYERD BAY

Coordinates: 55° 32′ N, 130° 51′ W

Primary entrance to Misty Fjords National Monument, this picturesque inlet east of Behm Canal is the waterway used by cruise ships to visit the monument.

SHRUBBY ISLAND AND BUSHY ISLAND

Coordinates: 56° 13′ N, 132° 57′ W

On the small islands in Snow Passage, west of Zarembo Island, you might spot sea lions up on the rocks. Named by Captain George Vancouver after Prince William's term as ranger of Bushy Park at Teddington.

TONGASS NARROWS

Coordinates: 55° 17′ N, 131° 36′ W (south entrance)

Waterway that separates Revilla and Gravina Islands. According to the Government Publications Librarian for the State Library of Alaska, the name possibly comes from Tlingit word for "People of the Island."

Along Tongass Narrows you will notice several old ships in various states of disrepair. On the Ketchikan side of the Narrows north of the Ketchikan Shipyard look for the Air Snipe; she is tied up along a small private pier just off Tongass Avenue. This sleek vessel was in service during World War II as a navy submarine chaser.

North of the Ketchikan Airport on Gravina Island look for the rusting blue hull of the Marine Bio Researcher; this ship was the last light ship in service at the mouth of the Columbia River. Her foremast held the light and the aft mast contained the fog horn. She was brought to Ketchikan in hope that her huge generator could be used for the production of electricity. Before being abandoned she was a research vessel.

The rusting hull just south of the mill on Gravina Island was a Navy seagoing salvage tug; she was built to pull battle ships.

TOTEM BIGHT
Coordinates: 55° 22' N, 131° 43' W

North of Ketchikan on Revilla Island, Totem Bight State Park contains the largest collection of totem poles in the state, many of them authentic reproductions. The clan house and some of the poles along the beach can be seen from the ship on the east side of Tongass Narrows.

WARD COVE
Coordinates: 55° 24' N, 131° 43' W

Small inlet on Tongass Narrows north of Ketchikan, Ward Cove was named for a gentleman who worked for the Hudson Bay Company. The cove is the former site of one of Ketchikan's largest employers, the Ketchikan Pulp Company which closed its doors in 1997. Some of the buildings are now being used by the Alaska Marine Highway System.

ZAREMBO ISLAND
Coordinates: 56° 20' N, 132° 52' W

East of Prince of Wales Island surrounded by Sumner Strait, Stikine Strait and Snow Passage, this island was named by Russians for Dionisii Zarembo, a naval officer. Because of having to slow down to navigate through Snow Passage, you can get a good chance to check out the beaches of Zarembo Island. In addition to possible bear and Sitka black-tailed deer, a herd of elk were introduced to the island a few years back and can frequently be seen.

CITIES AND TOWNS

JUNEAU

Coordinates: 58° 18′ N, 134° 25′ W
Population (2009):   31, 262

Located east of Douglas Island along Gastineau Channel, Juneau is the only United States capital city located on the mainland that cannot be reached by car. Named after prospector Joe Juneau, the town was made territorial capital in 1912, and later state capital 1959.

Founded by Dick Harris and Joe Juneau in 1880, the tent city was originally called Harrisburg. After some liquid persuasion, Joe Juneau convinced the town folk to change the name to Juneau – and Juneau it is today. Juneau was founded on gold; from the first strike on Gold Creek to the Treadwell Mine, largest gold mining operation of its time, gold fueled the economy of Juneau and the state until 1945 when the last mine closed. In its heyday there were seven major gold mines in operation in Juneau. You can still see what's left of the old A & J Mine under the Mt. Roberts Tramway.

Juneau became the official territorial capital in 1912, and later became the state capital. Today government is the economic backbone of the community, followed by tourism. The background of beautiful mountains and snow-clad peaks makes Juneau one of the most beautiful capital cities in the country. It is also the only capital with a glacier in its backyard; the Mendenhall Glacier is just 13 miles from the state capital building.

Juneau is located on the mainland. It is on the eastern shore of the Gastineau Channel. Directly behind town to the east, high in the Coast Mountains is the Juneau Icefield, an immense field of compact glacial ice that feeds over 37 different glaciers including the Mendenhall, Taku, Norris, and Hole-in-the Wall glaciers. To the west of Juneau is the town of Douglas, located on Douglas Island, it currently is connected to the mainland by a bridge but it is believed that one day it will be possible to drive between the two towns as so much glacial silt is filling in Gastineau Channel the water will soon be gone. Juneau is the gateway to many natural wonders: the Juneau Icefield, Mendenhall Glacier, the whales of Auke Bay, the bears of Taku Lodge, the trails and vistas of Mt. Roberts, and much more. The great thing is that it is all so easily accessible.

For those interested in exploring on foot, you can pick up a walking tour map prepared by the Convention and Visitors Bureau. There is an information booth located at the cruise pier next to the Mt. Roberts Tram and

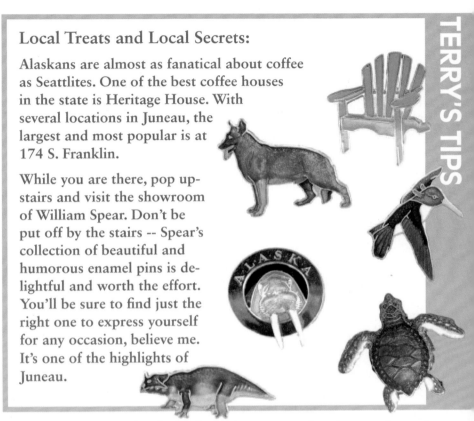

Local Treats and Local Secrets:

Alaskans are almost as fanatical about coffee as Seattlites. One of the best coffee houses in the state is Heritage House. With several locations in Juneau, the largest and most popular is at 174 S. Franklin.

While you are there, pop upstairs and visit the showroom of William Spear. Don't be put off by the stairs -- Spear's collection of beautiful and humorous enamel pins is delightful and worth the effort. You'll be sure to find just the right one to express yourself for any occasion, believe me. It's one of the highlights of Juneau.

the library. Before you head off take a minute to use the telescopes located near the pier; check out Mt. Juneau to the north of the city – you might see mountain goats. Once you are ready to move on, continue up Franklin Street past the shops and head uptown (and uphill.). Monday – Friday the state capital is open to the public for guided tours. Next door is the City Museum. Not far away on Calhoun is the Governor's Mansion. Back on 5th Street, you won't want to miss St. Nicholas' Russian Orthodox Church, oldest Russian orthodox church in Southeast. The octagonal building with a gold onion dome was built in 1894 in Siberia, disassembled, and rebuilt in Juneau. Juneau is also the home of the State Museum, at 395 Whittier. The museum has excellent natural as well as cultural history exhibits.

As you are heading back downtown, note the facades of the buildings, which reflect the city's pride as it blossomed with the responsibility of state government. However, some of the more rustic buildings date back to the boom times of the gold rush. In 1914, there were 30 bars on Franklin Street, which says a lot about the town's priorities back then. Today, the old Alaskan Hotel at 167 South Franklin, built in 1913, is one of the treasures of the city. The interior makes you feel like you've stepped back in time. Up the street, visit the Baranof Hotel to see an excellent example of Art Deco architecture in Alaska. Most people, however, want to visit the world famous Red Dog Saloon. The original Red Dog burned down, but the new building located across from the library is a fun place for locals and visitors alike. Not to be missed is the tram ride up Mt. Roberts, a corporation owned and operated by Native-Americans. Not only are the views spectacular, but there are trails, restaurants, an interpretive center, shops, and a movie about Tlingit history.

The Patsy Ann Statue

Before you leave Juneau make sure you stop by and touch the statue of Patsy Ann. In the 1930's, the locals named a deaf, homeless dog Patsy Ann; she showed up every day a ship tied up at the dock. Not only was she there, she was always waiting at the correct one of seven docks. In 1937, the mayor made her the "Official Greeter" of Juneau and exempted her from licensing. The statue of Patsy Ann was raised in loving memory of her.

TRACY ARM

Coordinates: 57° 50′ N, 133° 35′ W

For many years, Tracy Arm remained the secret paradise of locals who had the area to themselves. Tracy Arm is not a national or state park; it is an open, unregulated wilderness area. Little by little, smaller expeditionary ships began to include this storybook fjord in their itineraries. Now many larger ships prudently navigate the narrow waterway to offer their guests a chance to behold some of the most spectacular scenery in Southeast Alaska.

Like Misty Fjords, Tracy Arm is a glacially created valley that has been filled in by the sea. But unlike Misty Fjords, there is still an active glacier at the end of the fjord. Sawyer Glacier is not an exceptionally large glacier but it is known for producing very large, beautiful, deep blue ice bergs.

Every minute in Tracy Arm is spectacular. Upon arrival, weather permitting, you will be in view of Sumdum Glacier to the southeast or the starboard side of the ship. The name is a Tlingit name. Many years ago the

glacier touched the sea. Today it ends on dry land. You can spot the glacial ice by the crevasses and the ice color. To enter into Tracy Arm you must cross Holkham Bay. Your ship will round Harbor Island before making its approach into Tracy Arm. Off to the south, past Sumdum Glacier, is Endicott Arm. Like Tracy Arm it is also a fjord. The two bodies of water were named by Lieut. Commander H.B. Mansfield to honor Civil War military figure Benjamin Franklin Tracy, who was the Secretary of the Navy from 1889–1893, and William Endicott, who was Secretary of War from 1885–1889.

Tracy Arm is 29 miles in length, approximately 1.5 miles in width, and about 700 feet deep. So you can enjoy every minute of this magnificent waterway at your own pace, use the following information to guide you:

Shortly after crossing the bar is Mile 4 and Williams Cove. (Mile 4 = 4 miles from the bar.) This idyllic spot located on the north side of the fjord is a favorite for local sailors who often drop anchor overnight. Bergs from Sawyer Glacier beach themselves in the shallow water. Four miles up the fjord is Mile 9 and Big Bend; this is a hard-to-starboard turn. Once clearing the corner, the fjord opens out. On both the port and starboard side you can see textbook examples of glacially carved "U" shaped valleys. From many of them beautiful waterfalls form as melting snow and ice gather in glacially carved bowls.

Two of the largest are at Mile 12, Hole-in-the-Wall Falls, located on the port side, and Mile 14 and Icy Falls, on the starboard side. Farther down Mile 16 is Mud Flats. Since a fjord has no natural banks, the "beach" exposed at low tide is really a buildup of glacial silt accumulated from the nearby stream. Mud Flats is a favorite place for brown and black bear. Past Mud Flats there are deep glacial valleys on the south shore. On the north side of the fjord notice the sheer rock cliff. This is Mile 16, called The Wall. At this point your ship will make two turns known as the "S" Turns. After the first turn, straight ahead you will see the Rock Slide at Mile 20. As the name implies, it is a huge rock slide that looks like the entire face of the mountain was sliced off and slid into the sea. That is probably what happened. In the "freshly" exposed mountain side you can see the twisted strata of the Coast Mountains. You can see how the layers of rock buckled up forming the mountain range. Because the Pacific Plate is still slamming into the North American plate, the mountains are still growing, the earth is still shaking, and volcanoes are still rising. After the second turn the small island that will be in view at Mile 26 is Margarite or Sawyer Island. There is an active eagle's nest on the north side of the island. Margarite Island marks the point where the two branches of Sawyer Glacier can be seen.

Crossing the Bar

Notice the build-up of ice in front of the ship. It's as though these huge ice bergs have beached themselves on some hidden underwater wall. Well, that's exactly what has happened. The submerged moraine at the beginning of Tracy Arm is very high – it is known as "the bar." At low tide you can actually see the exposed top. Buoys mark the very narrow channel through which large ships must pass. During strong tidal periods, the current moves through very quickly creating whirlpools and eddies; sometimes the buoys may be pulled down under water. Don't be surprised if your ship tilts a little going through. If there is too much ice built up at the bar, your Captain may not be able to enter. In the end, it's all about safety.

Starting in 2008, cruise ships visiting Tracy Arm have been asked to observe the following guidelines as put forth by the Tongass National Forest Wilderness Best Management Practices for Tracy Arm-Fords Terror Wilderness. The following operations will be minimized:

Outside announcements to preserve the peace and quiet

Visible ship emissions to maintain clean air standards.

Unnecessary navigation that disturbs wildlife.

Sawyer Glacier begins in the Coast Mountains about 10 miles to the east. A solid peak of granite juts out, causing the glacier to split into two branches. The two branches follow very short and steep paths down to the sea. Sawyer Glacier is about 9.6 miles in length, and South Sawyer is about 14 miles. Both branches are retreating; look at the clean, bare sides of the mountains next to the edge of the glacier. You will be able to see that not too long ago the glacier was longer, wider, and higher. In front of South Sawyer the water is deeper and there is more room for a big ship. How much ice (bergs, growlers, brash, etc.) is in the water will determine how close to the glacier your Captain will be able to maneuver the ship. If you are visiting at the beginning of the summer, no doubt the ice floe will be full of harbor seals and their new pups. Look carefully for those crescent shapes on the ice. The sheer cliffs at the head of Tracy Arm are also ideal for mountain goats. Watch for those cream colored dots walking up the rock wall. Remember everything looks very small because you are still very far away. Be patient. It's all about proportion in Alaska.

SOUTH SAWYER GLACIER

Coordinates: 57° 51′ N, 133° 07′ W

Finally, Mile 29 is South Sawyer Glacier. This tidewater glacier is one of the most exciting to visit in all of the state because of the extraordinary blue color of the ice and the disproportionately large bergs that calve off. So why is this glacier so blue? And why are the bergs so big? Remember that the blue color of glacial ice is caused by the pressure of the ice compressing out the air, which changes the crystalline structure, thus allowing all the colors of the spectrum to be absorbed except blue which bounces around longest; the more compressed the ice the deeper the hue of blue. South Sawyer Glacier is traveling down a steep hillside. It is as though the glacier were going down a flight of steps; with each step it compresses onto itself, compounding the pressure. By the time it reaches water's edge – it's solid – and BLUE. Consequently, when it calves, the ice does not crumble and shower down: it cracks and discharges enormous blocks of ice. The bergs from South Sawyer glacier stay intact far down Tracy Arm, not only because they are big but also because they are solid, taking longer to melt. That is also why so many pile up at the bar. Those that do escape can float all the up the Gastineau Channel and beach themselves on Juneau's doorsteps. Hopefully during your trip to Tracy Arm you will see calving or some of the "shooters" for which Sawyer Glacier is so famous.

Kayakers like to camp on Margarite Island, thinking it is safe from bears. A few years ago some folks were rudely awakened by a juvenile black bear ravaging their packs. They did not know bears could swim. Surprise!

FACTS

LANDMARKS AND POINTS OF INTEREST

AUKE BAY

Cooordinates: 58° 24′ N, 134° 47′ W

Body of water to the north of Juneau and Douglas Island, south of the entrance to Lynn Canal. The sheltered waters of Auke Bay make it a favorite area for whales and whale-watchers.

AUKE LAKE

Coordinates: 58° 23′ N, 134° 42′ W

North of Juneau, Auke Lake is a favorite recreational area for locals. The name "auke" in Tlingit means lake – so Auke Lake is really "Lake Lake."

THE BROTHERS

Coordinates: 57° 17′ N, 133° 48′ W

Located in Frederick Sound at the southern end of Stephens Passage, the two islands of The Brothers are a favorite spot for humpback whales.

DOUGLAS ISLAND

Coordinates: 58° 16′ N, 134° 30′ W

Between Gastineau Channel and Stephens Passage, Douglas Island is the island across the channel from the city of Juneau. During the boom

days of the 1880's, thousands flocked to Juneau and the nearby town of Douglas. In the old days you had to row across the narrows of the Channel. One of the largest gold mines in the world, the Treadwell Mine, was located south of the town on Douglas Island. Today a bridge connects Juneau and Douglas. The island was named in 1794 by Captain George Vancouver for John Douglas, the Bishop of Salisbury, who edited the journals of Captain Cook's third voyage in which Vancouver sailed as mate.

ENDICOTT ARM

Coordinates: 57° 43′ N, 133° 29′ W

The southeast branch of Holkam Bay is Endicott Arm. Named after Secretary of War (1885 – 1889) William Endicott, the waterway is also a glacially created fjord.

5 FINGERS LIGHT HOUSE

Coordinates: 57° 16′ N, 133° 37′ W

Just east of The Brothers, Five Fingers Light House was originally built in 1904 and rebuilt in 1931, with the facility being automated in 1969.

FREDERICK SOUND (SOUTH)

Coordinates: 57° 07′ N, 133° 51′ W

South of Stephens Passages, Frederick Sound continues west/southwest to Sumner Strait.

GASTINEAU CHANNEL

Coordinates: 58° 13′ N, 134° 15′ W

The narrow body of water between Douglas Island and the mainland, Gastineau Channel is your entryway to the capital city of Juneau. The provenance of the name Gastineau is uncertain; it first appears on charts in Victoria, British Columbia. John Gastineau, a British citizen but resident of British Columbia, worked as a civil engineer in Alaska.

HARBOR ISLAND
Coordinates: 57° 45′ N, 133° 37′ W

Island located at the entrance of Holkam Bay.

HOLKAM BAY
Coordinates: 57° 45′ N, 133° 39′ W

East of Stephens Passage between Snettisham Peninsula and Sumdum
Peninsula, Holkam Bay marks the entry into Tracy and Endicott Arms.
Named in 1794 by Captain George Vancouver for a town in England.

JUNEAU ICEFIELD
One of the largest icefields in the state, the Juneau Icefield, located to
the east of the capital city, stretches over an area larger than the state of
Rhode Island and feeds over 37 glaciers.

MENDENHALL GLACIER

Coordinates: 58° 25′ N, 134° 31′ W

Named after W.C. Mendenhall of the U.S. Geological Survey, this 12 mile long glacier is not one of Alaska's largest, but because of its proximity to Juneau it is definitely one of the most popular. Just 13 miles from the state capital building, Mendenhall is the most visited glacier in the state. Many tours include a visit and if you are on a budget, for $1.50 the Capital Transit Lemon Creek/Mendenhall Valley city bus will get you about a mile from the Visitor's Center. A highlight is the new trail and platform that has been specifically constructed to allow visitors a chance to watch bears safely. There are several bear residents that regularly visit the area around the Visitor's Center. If you are sailing along Stephens Passage in daylight you can see Mendenhall Glacier north of Douglas Island to the east at the far end of Auke Bay.

PORT SNETTISHAM

Coordinates: 57° 59′ N, 133° 47′ W

A glacially carved inlet located north of Tracy Arm and south of Taku Inlet, the bay was named after Nicholas Styleman's home of Snettisham Hall. The main hydroelectric facility that supplies most of the power to Juneau is located up the northeast branch of Snettisham. Because of high winds that plague the area many of the power lines have been buried under ground and sea.

STEPHENS PASSAGE

Coordinates: 57° 56′ N, 133° 54′ W

The body of water between Admiralty Island and the mainland, it is approximately 80 miles in length and was named in 1794 by Captain George Vancouver for the Secretary to the British Admiralty, Sir Philip Stephens.

TAKU INLET

Coordinates: 58° 26′ N, 133° 57′ W

Northeast of the entrance to Gastineau Channel is Taku Inlet. This fjord is 32.8 miles long, from the Taku River that runs south from Canada to the mouth. The name comes from a Tlingit word, meaning wind, probably referring to the arctic blasts that wail down the river from the interior. Famous Taku winds have been known to reach 200 mph, causing residents of nearby Juneau to batten down everything that can fly. Previously there was a cannery on the site of the old Native American village. Today the highlight is a visit to the beautifully situated Taku Lodge.

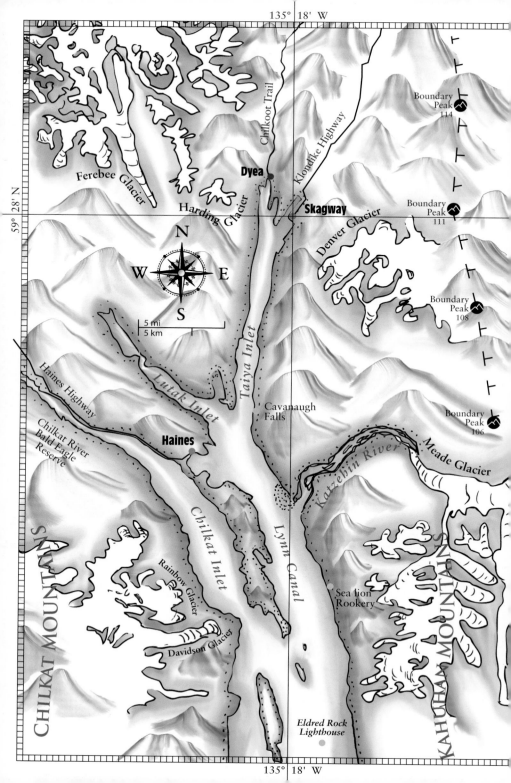

CRUISING
BEAUTIFUL LYNN CANAL

CITIES AND TOWNS

SKAGWAY

Coordinates: 59° 28′ N, 135° 18′ W

Population (2009):   870

Skagway is probably the hokiest town in Southeast Alaska, but, by far, it is the most fun! This tiny community of 870 year-round residents swells to 1,600 people when seasonal workers come up for the summer. Located on the northeast fork of Taiya Inlet, Skagway is the northernmost town in Southeast Alaska and was the gateway to the Yukon for hundreds of thousands of prospectors during the Klondike Gold Rush. The name in Tlingit means, "Place of the North Wind." In the summer the wind comes down Lynn Canal, making the climate warmer and drier than the rest of Southeast. Skagway residents take advantage of this and are known for their prolific flower gardens. Don't hesitate to admire. In the winter the cold, dry wind from the Yukon makes Skagway colder and snowier than the rest of Southeast.

As one of the two most popular routes available for prospectors to cross the mountains into the Yukon, Skagway at the base of the 43 mile long White Pass Trail became a boom town of the 1898 Klondike Gold Rush. Fourteen buildings dating back to that time have been preserved and are on the National Historic Register. Part of the town is included in the Klondike Gold Rush National Historical Park, which also includes the 33-mile-long Chilkoot Trail, and parts of Pioneer Square in downtown Seattle. There is a National Park Service office in the old Assayer's Office near the train station. Rangers give walking tours of town and documentaries are shown regularly in the small theater, free of charge.

Who really shot Soapy Smith?

The story of how Frank Reid shot Soapy Smith on July, 8 1898, is part of Skagway legend. Whenever there is an ear to listen someone will obligingly tell the tale of how an angry and inebriated Soapy Smith heard that Frank Reid was conspiring against him and marched down to the wharf where the shooting took place. But some historians say, 'not so fast,' for Reid wasn't the only one at the wharf. There were four other men standing guard in front of the building where a meeting of the vigilante group, the Committee of 101, was taking place. This has been well documented by one of them, J. Tanner, who later became a U.S. Deputy Marshal. According to Jeff Smith, great grandson of Soapy Smith, letters from his great-grandmother Mary, as well as documents from Deputy Tanner, reveal that after the initial encounter between Reid and Smith, Reid was knocked unconscious. One of the guards, Jesse Murphy, grabbed Soapy's rifle and shot him in the chest, killing him instantly. Given the state of the justice system or the lack there of in Skagway, it was decided that the "official story" would be that Smith and Reid shot at each other in self-defense rather than risk a drawn out trial or the retribution of the vigilantes. It was self-defense.

FACTS

In the summer of 1889, thousands of people were camped out on the mud flats. The town was run by thugs and thieves like Soapy Smith. Jefferson "Soapy" Smith came to Skagway from Leadville, Colorado, where he earned his nickname from selling thousands of bars of Sopalion soap which he planted with $100 bills. After being run out of town, he headed north to Alaska. Arriving in Skagway he made himself out to be a fair and compassionate guy: he started a shelter for abandoned dogs, got himself elected mayor, and managed to open several bars, brothels, and gambling halls. After Soapy became sheriff, all hell broke loose. People cheated and robbed by Soapy's men had no recourse as Soapy was now the sheriff. In protest, Frank Reid organized a group called the Committee of 101. They intercepted Soapy and shot him dead. Reid was fatally wounded. The townsfolk honored Reid by erecting a monument to him in the Klondike Gold Rush cemetery. No honors for Soapy; the town didn't even want him buried within the cemetery. So, the grave was dug outside the grounds. Now, however, since the cemetery continued to grow, Soapy's grave is at the cemetery entrance and his is the first name you see!

Because the White Pass was purportedly traversable by pack animals, thousands of horses lost their lives on the narrow trail, giving it the nickname the Dead Horse Trail. However, the pass was lower in elevation by 600 feet than nearby Chilkoot, and in 1898 construction was started on a narrow-gauge railroad under the leadership of Michael J. Heney. It took 26 months and 10 million dollars, but with British financing, US engineers and Canadian labor, the White Pass and Yukon Railway began service in 1900. Even though the Gold Rush was officially over, the existence of the

railroad kept alive many communities including Skagway. Less fortunate was nearby Dyea at the head of the Chilkoot Trail; it became a ghost town and officially closed its post office in 1906. Today you can still ride the White Pass & Yukon Railroad in cars that were originally constructed at the roundhouse in Skagway in the 1900's. The track follows the White Pass and the views are magnificent. No trip to Skagway is complete without experiencing this bit of history.

Walk down Broadway to see the historic Red Onion Saloon, the Golden North Hotel, and the Arctic Brotherhood, decorated with thousands of pieces of driftwood. It was said that to be member of the Arctic Brotherhood you had to cross the Chilkoot or White Pass and return to talk about it. Excellent pieces from Skagway's historic past can be seen at the Trail of '98 Museum as well as the National Parks Service Visitor's Center. About one mile out of town is the Gold Rush Cemetery where Soapy Smith is buried.

For those wanting a good hike, the trail to Dewey Lakes will provide a moderate workout. To get to the trailhead cross Congress Street from Pullen Park and follow the railroad tracks; there are signs on your left.

Local Treats

After all that walking you might work up an appetite or just want a snack. If all you desire is a cold one, there are plenty of fun places for a beer. Skagway has its own brewing company; first started in 1897, the Skagway Brewing Company was resurrected in 1997.

But Skagway is known for its assortment of delicious little cafes and bakeries. If you are hungry, the Sweet Tooth on 315 Broadway is an institution. They have a hard ice cream soda fountain for a great malt or milkshake. Their halibut burgers are local favorites. The Skagway Fish Company, right up from the cruise ships on Congress Street, is a close and popular place.

If you need a Starbuck's the first one in all of Southeast Alaska is right here at Excelsior Cafe. Don't miss the fresh baked pastries and homemade sandwiches and of course your venti, mocha, skinny, or frappachino latte.

TERRY'S TIPS

Another less strenuous walk is to head out south of the airport to the Skagway River where you can cross via the pedestrian bridge, and continue up the Par Course trail to Smuggler's Cove.

The graffiti on the wall next to the Railroad Dock (or cruise pier), dates back to the days of the Gold Rush. The first thing painted on the wall was said to have been the skull of Soapy Smith. From that time on the wall became a billboard upon which merchants advertised their stores and sailors posted the colors of their ships. When cruise ships started calling on Skagway they too engaged in the tradition. On its maiden voyage the insignia of the ship and name of her captain are painted on the hillside. The oldest markings are from the ships of the Canadian Pacific Line; *Princess Adelaide*, *Princess Louise*, *Princess Norah* 1928, and *Princess Charlotte* 1929. Look closely and you will see names from the not-too-distant-past, like Royal Viking, Chandris, and Regency. That tradition continues today, so try to find your ship on the wall, as well as my name!

Skagway and nearby Haines are the only two communities in Southeast Alaska to which you can drive. The Klondike Highway connects Skagway with Whitehorse, Yukon Territory. During the summer Skagway is filled with motor homes and campers.

During the winter of 2008/2009, using money collected off a Skagway city tax, the cruise pier area at the railroad dock was greatly improved. There now are two restroom facilities, one at the end of the pier and one in Pullen Park, as well as wider sidewalks, lovely landscaping, and helpful signage. Though the walk to town is only ½ mile, there is a shuttle service available from the head of the pier. Pick-up is ongoing and there is a nominal charge. For the romantic you can hire a horse drawn buggy to see Skagway in style.

Real estate bargain

Everyone wants to find a great real estate deal, right? You need look no further – buy Skagway! If you would have bought beachfront property during the Gold Rush you would have gained six feet of land today. The reason? Glacial rebounding! The Skagway Valley was under a huge sheet of ice for thousands of years compressing the land; now that the ice is gone it is swelling back up at a rate of .76 inches a year!

HAINES

Coordinates:	59° 14' N, 135° 26' W
Population (2010):	2,400

Whenever the perfect picture of Alaska is sought, an image of Haines is usually chosen. It is the most picturesque community in Alaska. The storybook-like town nestled at the base of the majestic Chilkat Mountains is 16.3 miles down Taiya Inlet. When leaving Skagway you can see Haines on the starboard side about one hour after departure. Its buildings look like toys against the towering snow-clad peaks. Though Skagway and Haines are only about 15 minutes apart by plane, or 45 minutes away by water taxi, it takes 8 hours to drive between the two. To get from Skagway to Haines, motorists must take the Klondike Highway north into Canada, proceed toward Whitehorse, and then head to the southwest along the Haines Highway. However you arrive, it is worth the effort.

Long before the white man arrived, Haines was home of the Chilkat Tlingit. Known for their finely woven blankets, the Chilkats have always been considered great artists among the Tlingits. Chilkat blankets are woven from the wool of the under-belly of a mountain goat. Fibers from cedar root were used for the warp. Colors were created from natural dyes in shades of cream, yellow, teal, and black. Today the Chilkats are revitalizing their cultural arts through the Alaska Indian Arts Center of Haines. Here craftsmen and artists from throughout the state carve, work silver, weave, make baskets, and engage in storytelling. The Alaska Indian Arts Center is home to the Chilkat Dancers, a troupe of Tlingit dancers who have won international acclaim performing around the world.

After Alaska became a territory, military presence was needed. Fort William Seward was opened in 1904, and remained the first and only military installation in the territory until the outbreak of World War II. Though isolated, the fort was a showplace with beautiful quarters for the officers and state of the art facilities. To avoid confusion with other "Seward" addresses, it was renamed Chilkoot Barracks in 1922. But the name was changed back in to Fort William Seward in 1972 when it was designated a National Historical Landmark. The fort was decommissioned in 1946. In 1947, a group of retirees bought up the buildings. The hospital became the home of the Alaska Indian Arts Center, now located at 13 Fort Seward Drive. Performances by the Chilkat Dancers can now be seen at the new Chilkat Center for the Arts Storytelling Theater which formerly was the Entertainment and Recreation Hall. The beautiful officers' quarters located around the parade ground were turned into private residences. The bachelor officers' quarters and the Commanding Officer's quarters became the Halsingland Hotel. Approaching Haines from the sea, you can see the symmetry of the buildings and orderliness of the present day community, a reminder of its service as a military post. Walking tour maps are available in most shops, museums, and visitors' information centers.

From the pier, it is an easy walk up the hill to the former fort. Many homes along the way have been turned into shops and galleries. Haines is home to well-known artists, photographers and writers, who no doubt gather inspiration from the majestic scenery. You can stroll through the streets and visit the Halsingland Hotel. A 20 minute walk down Beach Road will take you into the new section of town. Here you'll find more restaurants and bars. Taxis are available.

Among the many things for which Haines is known, most visitors come to experience the Chilkat River Bald Eagle Reserve. The Chilkat River does not freeze in the winter; consequently, it hosts a late-season run of salmon.

Knowing this, thousands of eagles winter over along the Chilkat each year. It becomes the greatest concentration of eagles in North America. Hundreds of eagles remain year-round making it an excellent place for bird watching. Along the river, too, you may see Sitka black tailed deer, moose, and occasionally, bears. If eagles are your passion, you won't want to miss the American Bald Eagle Foundation. Located two blocks from town, the foundation is dedicated to preserving and protecting eagles and their native habitat.

For museum lovers the Sheldon Museum and Cultural Center contains a small but very good collection of local artifacts. Many of the pieces here are one of a kind. Also, Haines has a Hammer Museum with 1000 hammers on display.

Shipwreck!

FACTS

When cruising along the placid waters of the Inside Passage during the long, lazy days of summer, it is hard to imagine how turbulent and dangerous these areas can be in the winter. Violent storms have taken many a ship in Southeast Alaska. One of the most infamous incidents was the sinking of the *Princess Sophia*, one of the Canadian Pacific Line ships. It was October 1918, and the 245 foot long, 2,320 ton ship was heading south down Lynn Canal with 353 passengers and crew when a blinding snow storm with strong northerly winds took her up onto Vanderbilt Reef. Due to the unrelenting storm the decision was made not to lower the life boats. It was later reported that the winds had reached 100 mph and the waves were at 30 feet. For over 40 hours she sat fast on the reef. The incoming tide and the continuing storm lifted her stern and swung the ship around on the reef, tearing out her hull. As water started to rush in the ship's boiler exploded, killing most onboard. Of the remaining passengers none survived save an English setter who swam to shore and was found 12 miles away.

DYEA

Coordinates: 59° 29' N, 135° 21' W

Population (2010):   0

Located on the northwest fork of the Taiya Inlet, Dyea in 1898 was a bustling boom town at the head of the Chilkoot Trail. After the gold rush, the decision to bring the White Pass-Yukon Railroad down the wider, lower White Pass to Skagway made Dyea obsolete. The town became a ghost town. Today what is left of Dyea is preserved as part of the Klondike National Historical Monument, which includes the Chilkoot Trail. You can walk among what is left of the town, hike a portion of the Chilkoot trail, and visit the Slide Cemetery where those who were killed in the Palm Sunday Avalanche of 1898 are buried.

SCENIC SAILING

ELDRED ROCK LIGHT HOUSE
Coordinates: 58° 56' N, 135° 13' W

One of the most photographed and painted lighthouses in Alaska, Eldred Rock Lighthouse is located on Lynn Canal approximately 42 miles south of Skagway (2.5 hours after departure). The octagonal lighthouse was built in 1906, and converted to an unmanned light in 1973. The island was named in 1880 by Marcus Baker in honor of his wife, Sarah Eldred. It is the only original standing lighthouse in Alaska.

KATZEHIN RIVER/MEADE GLACIER
Coordinates: 59° 12' N, 135° 16' W

The silty water of the Katzehin River empties into Lynn Canal across from the town of Haines, approximately 20 miles south of Skagway. The huge brown fan that pushes out into the clean water of the canal is from the glacial silt carried by the melt water off Meade Glacier. Meade Glacier is far to the northeast, but the volume of melt water is what forms the Katzehin River. Watch for the change in the water on the port side as you sail from Skagway about 1 hour after departure.

PT. SHERMAN LIGHT HOUSE
Coordinates: 58° 52' N, 135° 15' W

Lighthouse located on Lynn Canal south of Comet, 6 miles south of Eldred Rock.

RAINBOW AND DAVIDSON GLACIERS

Coordinates: 59° 05' N, 135° 26' W

About 1 ½ hours after departure from Skagway (30 minutes from Haines), you will see two glaciers on the starboard side, Rainbow Glacier and Davidson. About 22 miles south of Skagway, these glaciers have their source in the surrounding Chilkat Mountains. Rainbow Glacier is a hanging glacier; Davidson Glacier is a valley glacier. Not long ago, Davidson was a tidewater glacier, but it has retreated from the water's edge and continues to shrink drastically every year. As you pass you can see how the sides of the glacier are thinning away from the edge of the mountain. Out in front of the terminus is a ring of trees growing on an ancient terminal moraine left by the glacier. They encircle a fresh water lake created by the melt of the glacier. Canoe excursions are available from your tour desk.

SEA LIONS

Coordinates: 59° 10' N, 135° 15' W

On the east shore (port side) of Lynn Canal, about 1 hour 40 min. south of Skagway, past the mouth of the Katzehin River, a large colony of Steller sea lions can often be seen through mid-summer. This rookery contains up to 300 sea lions that haul out onto the rocks to enjoy the warm rays of the afternoon sun. Because it is such a treat to see them, many ships will detour close to shore to give you a better look. Ship's officers know not to bring the ship too close or cause too much disturbance as this can potentially irritate the sea lions. Cruise ships work closely with local authorities to ensure the balance between industry and nature. The sea lions are monitored by the University of Alaska; notice the solar panel powering a small camera that observes the rookery.

LANDMARKS AND POINTS OF INTEREST

CHILKAT ISLANDS
Coordinates: 59° 03′ N, 135° 16′ W

Small group of islands south of Seduction Point; good spot for whale watching.

CHILKOOT TRAIL
Coordinates: 59° 29′ N, 135° 20′ W

The second of two choices for 1898 prospectors, the Chilkoot Trail was 32 miles in length but the terrain was steep and treacherous. Being shorter, it was faster, and for many became the trail of choice. Today it is part of the Klondike Gold Rush National Monument and is open to the public. To get to the trail head take the Dyea Road out 7.5 miles west. Hikers can hike the trail across the summit; picks, shovels, carts, boxes, boots, etc. from the Gold Rush can still be seen. As it is a living museum everything must be left as it is.

HARDING GLACIER
Coordinates: 59° 27′ N, 135° 23′ W

Directly to the south across the Taiya Inlet from Skagway, you will see a peak with the tell-tale signs of glacial ice. The crevasses and the blue color of the ice that pushes over the rim of the mountain should tell you that it's a glacier. It is a small but significant glacier. Harding Glacier was named after President Warren G. Harding who was the first US President to visit Alaska.

KENSINGTON GOLD MINE
Coordinates: 58° 50′ N, 134° 60′ W

The most recent gold mine to open in Alaska, portions of the mine can be seen on the east side of Lynn Canal about 4 hours after leaving Skagway. Originally staked during the 1880 Juneau Gold Rush, the mine was closed until recent improvements in mining technology.

171

LYNN CANAL
Coordinates: 58° 32' N, 135° 02' W

Though named a canal, Lynn Canal is really a fjord with an average depth
of 1,700 feet, making it is one of the deepest in the world. It was named in
1794 by Captain George Vancouver; overwhelmed by its natural beauty,
he named the waterway after his home of King's Lynn. Lynn Canal is 87
miles long, reaching Chatham Strait and Stephens Passage in the south.

SEDUCTION POINT
Coordinates: 59° 05' N, 135° 17' W

Located south of Haines and to the east of Davidson Glacier, Seduction
Point hems in Chilkat Inlet. Story has it that the land was given its name
from a local Tlingit custom. Traditionally when the Tlingits were not busy
fishing they had time to trade and/or raid nearby villages. Upon hearing
that a raiding canoe was nearing, the villagers would gather up their fair-
est women, who would strip. Parading up and down the beach they hoped
to lure the raiding party ashore where they would be ambushed by the
village's warriors. It is said this tactic was tried on Capt. Vancouver, who
resisted the trick but named the point for the attempt.

SENTINEL LIGHTHOUSE

Coordinates: 58° 30′ N, 134° 53′ W

Located on Lynn Canal, 30 miles south of Eldred Rock.

TAIYA INLET

Coordinates: 59° 27′ N, 135° 18′ W

Northernmost reach of Lynn Canal; divided into two branches, the north-west fork ends in Dyea, the northeast fork in Skagway.

WHITE PASS

Coordinates: 59° 29′ N, 135° 16′ W

One of two choices prospectors had in 1898, for traversing the Coast Mountains into Canada's Yukon Territory. The White Pass is 40 miles long and lower in elevation than the nearby Chilkoot Trail. Today the historic White Pass & Yukon Railroad constructed from 1898 – 1900, parallels the White Pass, and has been designated an International Historic Civil Engineering Landmark along with the Panama Canal and the Eiffel Tower.

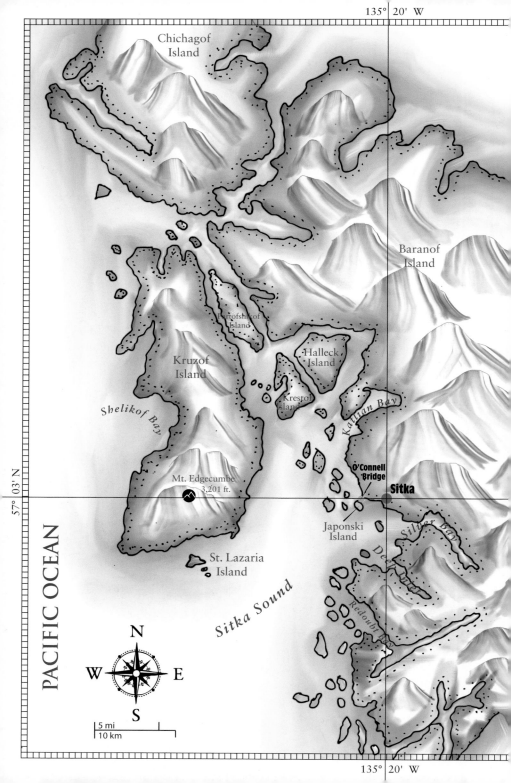

CITIES AND TOWNS

SITKA

Coordinates: 57° 03′ N, 135° 20′ W

Population (2004):   8,805

Known as the "Paris of the Pacific," Sitka was founded by the Russians in 1799. A charter granted by Emperor Paul I established the Russian-American Trading Company, led by Alesander Baranof. Originally the site of a Shee-atka Tlingit village, the first attempts at settling the area by Europeans met with resistance. The town was burned in 1802 and re-established in 1804. Sitka became the first territorial capital of Alaska from 1867 – 1912. Located on Baranof Island, Sitka still retains its Russian flavor. It is the only community in Southeast Alaska that faces the open sea. Nestled at the far end of Sitka Sound, the town is sheltered from severe weather. Hundreds of small rocks and islands dot Sitka Sound, many of them named by the early Russian settlers. If Mother Nature is cooperative, you can see Mt. Edgecumbe. Located at the northwest entrance to Sitka Sound on Kruzof Island is Mt. Edgecumbe (3,201 feet), an extinct volcano. It last erupted 8,000 years ago.

A few years ago practical jokers set tires on fire within the caldera of Mt. Edgecumbe causing white smoke to billow out. Locals waking that 1st day of April 1974, were not amused as the volcano is just 16 miles from town. A Coast Guard helicopter was sent out to survey the area. Once the prank was revealed the perpetrators spent April Fool's Day in jail!

Your ship will be anchored between Baranof Island and the Channel Islands. The harbor is not deep enough to accommodate large ships so all large cruise ships must anchor. There are two tender piers: one is in Crescent Harbor, and the other is under the O'Connell Bridge. As you approach either tender pier you will see the O'Connell Bridge. It is the first cable-stayed girder-spanned bridge in the United States. It is a very sleek and modern bridge that contrasts with the traditional flavor of the town. The bridge links Baranof Island with Japonski Island. During World War II, Japonski Island was a naval air base. Gun mounts can still be seen on many of the Channel Islands. After the war the airfield was turned into a commercial airport now named the Rocky Guiterrez Airport. The Coast Guard occupies old navy buildings.

The onion dome of St. Michael's Russian Orthodox Church dominates the skyline. The church was first built in 1848; the dome was made from malachite. In 1966, a fire destroyed the church, but luckily the priceless icons were saved. Legend has it that one man single-handedly removed the 100 pound chandelier, which later took four men to replace. Using the original Russian building plans, the church was reconstructed as an exact replica. The original chandelier and icons are displayed in the church.

At the top of the Crescent Harbor tender pier is Centennial Hall where the New Archangel Dancers perform. This troupe of local dancers has captured the spirit of Russia in the Americas. Within the building is also the Isabele Miller Museum, a popular city museum. Next door is the Sitka Library, where you can sign up to use the free internet.

Sitka is a great port for walking. At the parking lot of the small boat harbor, Harbor Drive meets Lincoln Avenue. Across the street in the historic Hanlon-Osbakken House is the Sitka Rose Gallery, which contains an excellent collection of work by some of my favorite local artists. Just behind the gallery is Wintersong Soaps. Started by a mom who wanted a way to work from home, this cottage industry has become one of the most popular in Southeast Alaska. For both men and women, Wintersong has a wide range of soaps and bath products featuring local plants and traditional formulas. Two blocks down Lincoln to the south is the Russian Bishops House. Built in 1842, the building is on the National Historic Register. National Park Rangers guide you through. It is the oldest Russian building that is still standing in Alaska and is one of the four oldest Russian structures in the United States. From the Russian Bishop's House continue down Lincoln Street to Sheldon Jackson College. Dr. Sheldon Jackson was the Director of Education for the Alaskan territory from 1895 – 1900. Though the private liberal arts college has fallen on hard times and no longer offers classes, the Sheldon Jackson Museum is still open and worth a stop. Some say it is better than the State Museum in Juneau.

Continue farther down on Lincoln Street until you reach the Sitka National Historical Park. The park is a beautiful wooded area that was the original site of the final battle between the Tlingit and the Russians. There is an interpretive center with exhibits. Often Native wood carvers or weavers are on-site to demonstrate their skills. Documentaries on the battle are also shown. Beyond the historical significance of the area, today it houses

Local Treats

If you like sushi, you will love Sitka's Little Tokyo. On 315 Lincoln across from the Wells Fargo bank, this is the freshest, most tasty sushi you will have east of Japan. I once traced a line of ice water from a bucket full of fish taken straight off a fishing boat into the restaurant. It doesn't get much fresher than that!

a collection of some of the most beautiful totem poles in all Southeast Alaska. Starting with the display outside the Visitors Center, follow the trails through the park to discover more. Situated among their growing ancestors, these cedar poles have been carved and raised to remind admirers of the Tlingit past. Trails wind through dense forest filled with towering ferns, proof this is temperate rainforest. A salmon creek runs through the park and in late summer is filled with thousands of spawning fish.

Beyond the Sitka National Historical Park is the Alaska Raptor Center. This all-volunteer non-profit organization has become a leader in raptor rehabilitation and education. Between 100 and 200 injured birds are helped each year. The Center is open to the public. Visitors from all over the world have sponsored or "adopted" birds that have been rehabilitated and released back into the wild. Birds unable to return to their natural habitat have found a welcome home at the Center where they are ambassadors for their species, raising the awareness of visitors who meet them each year.

Lincoln Street is Sitka's downtown. It is filled with offices, shops and restaurants. Behind the businesses is Castle Hill. This small promontory was used by the Tlingit as a strategic lookout point. Later the Russians built many different buildings upon the same location. In 1837, Alesander Baranof built his sumptuous home nicknamed Baranof's Castle. On October 18, 1867, it was used for the transference of ownership of the Alaskan territory from Russia to the United States. The Castle burned in 1898.

In 1934, the first Alaska Pioneer Home was built in Sitka. Located on the Russian parade grounds, the home was and is one of the first retirement communities of its kind. There is a small gift store inside and visitors are welcome. Just behind the Pioneer House is the replica of the old Russian Blockhouse used to segregate the Tlingit from the Russians. Across Katlain Street, is Totem Square which contains a Tlingit totem pole carved with a Russian double-headed eagle. The city park also has a Russian cannon and several anchors. Benches look out over the boat harbor.

Many of you will tender into the O'Connell Lighter Pier. This facility, located under the O'Connell Bridge off Harbor Street, provides easy access to Totem Square and downtown Sitka. Smaller expeditionary cruise ships can dock at the end of Lincoln Street.

Next to the Pioneer House on Katlain Street is the Sheet' ka Kwaan Naa Khadi Tribal Community House, operated by the Sitka Tribal Association. The community house was built to resemble a traditional clan house. It features dancers in full regalia and a gift shop with locally made goods. The house itself is worth a visit just for the "Lovebirds" house screen, depicting the raven and eagle moieties. It is the largest of its kind in Southeast Alaska. The Tribal Association also operates the Visitor Transit, which shuttles visitors to all of Sitka's major downtown attractions.

If you happen to be on a ship that calls on Sitka in the early spring and/ or late fall, a walk down to Whale Park would be worthwhile. This new city park, located about 6 miles south of town, is a great place to view humpbacks. There are telescopes and hydrophones available along the boardwalk.

LANDMARKS AND POINTS OF INTEREST

ADMIRALTY ISLAND
Coordinates: 57° 59' N, 134° 34' W

Third largest island in Southeast Alaska, Admiralty Island is located between Chatham Strait and Stephens Passage. It is 96 miles long and contains 1,664 square miles of land including a one-million-acre reserve to preserve and protect brown bears. It is said there are more brown bears on Admiralty Island than all the Lower 48 United States combined. Admiralty was named in 1794, by Captain George Vancouver, in honor of the Royal Navy that sponsored his expedition.

BARANOF ISLAND
Coordinates: 57° 17′ N, 135° 10′ W

Known collectively as the A,B,C Islands, (Admiralty, Baranof, Chichagof), Baranof Island is the fourth largest island in Southeastern Alaska at 1,607 square miles. It is 105 miles long and the home of the city of Sitka. The island was named in 1805 by Russian Captain Lisianski in honor of the head of the Russian-American Trading Company, Alesander Baranof

CAPE DECISION LIGHT HOUSE
Coordinates: 56° 00′ N, 135° 42′ W

Original lighthouse was built in 1932, and later retrofitted to be un-manned. Located at the tip of Kuiu Island between Chatham Strait and Sumner Strait, Cape Decision was named in 1793 by Captain George Vancouver after deciding no Spanish explorers had surveyed this far north.

CHANNEL ISLANDS
Coordinates: 57° 02′ N, 135° 21′ W

The small islands directly in front of the city of Sitka are the Channel Islands. Your ship will be anchored between Baranof Island and these picturesque islands. Many contain beautiful vacation homes and cabins – accessible only by boat or sea plane. On the west side of the islands you still can see gun mounts set up by the Navy to protect the bay during World War II.

CHATHAM STRAIT
Coordinates: 56° 22′ N, 134° 28′ W (mouth)

Southeast from Baranof Island north to Lynn Canal, Chatham Strait was charted and named in 1794 by Captain George Vancouver to honor the Earl of Chatham.

CHICHAGOF ISLAND

Coordinates: 57° 48′ N, 135° 55′ W

Second largest island in Southeast Alaska at 2,104 square miles; Chichagof Island is north of Baranof Island between Chatham Strait to the east, Peril Strait to the south, Icy Strait to the north, and the Pacific to the west. It was named in 1805 by Russian Captain Lisianski.

JAPONSKI ISLAND

Coordinates: 57° 03′ N, 135° 21′ W

Located between Baranof Island and Kruzof Islands, Japonski is the largest of the Channel Islands. During World War II it was the site of the area's naval air station. After the war the buildings were used by the Coast Guard. It is also the home of the international airport as well as the campus of the University of Alaska Sitka.

ST. LAZARIA ISLAND

Coordinates: 56° 59′ N, 135° 42′ W

Small island south of Kruzof Island. Ships occasionally pass between the two islands on their way north. Look for sea lions on the rocks and a large colony of sea birds, including puffins, on the northwest side.

KRUZOF ISLAND

Coordinates: 57° 14′ N, 135° 42′ W

Located to the north of the entrance to Sitka Sound and west of Baranof Island, Kruzof Island was named in 1805 by Russian Captain Lisianski. Dominating the 27 mile long island is the extinct volcanic cone of Mt. Edgecombe.

MT. EDGECUMBE

Elevation: 3,201 feet
Coordinates: 57° 03′ N, 135° 45′ W

Located on Kruzof Island, Mt. Edgecumbe is an extinct volcano located

182

on Kruzof Island. It last erupted about 8,000 years ago, sending ash throughout the area. The volcano was named by Captain James Cook in 1778 after Lord Edgecumbe.

O'CONNELL BRIDGE
Coordinates: 57° 03' N, 135° 21' W

This sleek futuristic bridge was the first single-stayed, girder-spanned bridge in the United States. It unites downtown Sitka with Japonski Island, location of Sitka's airport.

SILVER BAY
Coordinates: 56° 59' N, 135° 32' W

Tranquil inlet southeast of Sitka on Sitka Sound, the old pier in Silver Bay may be the future home of Sitka's first deep water cruise ship terminal.

SITKA SOUND
Coordinates: 56° 59' N, 135° 30' W

Sheltered from the Pacific, Sitka Sound is nestled between Baranof Island and Kruzof Island. Within the Sound are numerous small rocks and islands including the Channel Islands.

135° 45' W

FAIRWEATHER

Grand Pacific Glacier

Ferris Glacier

Rendu Glacier

Cushing Glacier

Morse Glacier

Muir Glacier

Riggs Glacier

Carroll Glacier

McBride Glacier

Casement Glacier

Margerie Glacier

Mt. Abdallah
5,964 ft.

Rendu Inlet

Queen Inlet

Wachusett Inlet

Muir Inlet

Adams Inlet

Mt. Fairweather
15,300 ft.

Tarr Inlet

Russell
Island

Johns Hopkins Inlet

Lamplugh Glacier

Mt. Salisbury
12,000 ft.

Johns Hopkins Glacier

Reid Glacier

Muir
Point

Mt. Abbe
8,750 ft.

Glacier Bay

Mt. Orville
10,490 ft.

MOUNTAINS

Mt. Crillon
12,726 ft.

Geikie Inlet

Drake
Island

Mt. Bertha
10,240 ft.

Mt. La Perouse
10,728 ft.

BRADY
ICEFIELD

Willoughby
Island

Beardslee
Island

La Perouse Glacier

Icy
Point

Brady Glacier

Bartlett Cove
(Visitors Center)

Palma Bay

Gustavus

Dundas Bay

Icy Strait

GLACIER BAY
NATIONAL PARK

N

W   E

S

Taylor Bay

Lemesurier
Island

10 mi
10 km

Cape Spencer
Lighthouse

Inian
Islands

Point
Adolphus

Elfin Cove

Idaho Inlet

Cross Sound

Cape
Bingham

Lisianski Inlet

PACIFIC OCEAN

58° 24' N

135° 45' W

CRUISING
GLACIER BAY

CITIES AND TOWNS

BARTLETT COVE

Coordinates:	58° 26′ N, 135° 53′ W
Population (2005):	9

Located on the eastern mouth of Glacier Bay, Bartlett Cove is the head-quarters of Glacier Bay National Park, and contains the park's visitor center. The park is open from mid-May through mid-September. Most employees live in the nearby town of Gustavus; only nine people reside within the park all year.

GUSTAVUS

Coordinates:	58° 24′ N, 135° 45′ W
Population (2005):	429

Located at the eastern mouth of Glacier Bay, north of Icy Straits, the town of 429 year-round residents has an airport that serves locals as well as employees and visitors to the national park. Named for Swedish King Gustavus II.

HOONAH

Coordinates:	58° 07′ N, 135° 26′ W
Population (2000):	860

Located in Port Frederick the town of Hoonah is 70% Tlingit. They rely primarily on commercial fishing, canning and now tourism. Several cruise ships stop in Hoonah for a traditional salmon bake.

GLACIER BAY
Coordinates: 58° 24′ N, 135° 57′ W

The history of Glacier Bay is almost as impressive as the park. The first European to record the area was Captain George Vancouver. Looking for the Northwest Passage in 1791, he was commissioned to explore every inlet and waterway along the North Pacific Coast. From the area known as Icy Straits, so named by earlier Russian explorers, he tried to sail to the north, but was stopped by a wall of ice that was 20 miles wide and 4,000 feet thick. In 1879, just 88 years later, when John Muir first visited the same spot the wall of ice had retreated 48 miles to the north. In a little over 200 years, that wall of ice has retreated 65 miles. The huge depression where the ice once sat has been filled in by the sea that created Glacier Bay. Today the remnant of that great glacial system is divided into 12 tidewater glaciers.

In 1879, John Muir wanted to test the theory, first proposed in 1840 by Louis Agassiz, that the earth at one time experienced an Ice Age. Muir, who knew every inch of his beloved Sierra Nevada Mountains, could not account for the difference between the jagged peaks of the high elevations and the rounded appearance of the foothills. Using Agassiz's theory, he hypothesized that maybe during that Ice Age the great sheet of ice reached down as far as California. Those peaks that were tall enough to be free of the weight of the ice remained sharp and serrated; the lower elevations were rounded down, leaving deep U-shaped valleys. He came to Alaska to test the theory, as it was the closest place with active, accessible glaciers. He went to the same place cited by Vancouver. There he camped out on the ice, where he discovered, after many harrowing adventures, that the theory was true. Muir wrote about his time in Alaska in the still popular book, *Travels in Alaska*.

In 1925, 3.3 million acres in Glacier Bay were set aside as a National Monument. In 1980, it was re-designated a National Park. UNESCO declared the park a Biosphere Reserve in 1986; and, in 1992, Glacier Bay was listed as World Heritage Site. As a National Park, visits by cruise ships are regulated by the Park Service. Lots are drawn each year to see which ships will call, and when. At the mouth of the park in Bartlett Cove, two National Park Rangers responsible for your interpretive program will board by pilot boat. Depending on conditions within the park, they will work with the Captain and the pilots to determine the best thing to see for

that day. Some areas may be off limits due to ice, unstable conditions, or wildlife.

As the majority of the glaciers in Glacier Bay National Park are retreating, one of the most important aspects of research in the park is the study of plant succession in the wake of a retreating ice. Though these subtle changes are hard to detect from the decks of your ship, notice the difference between the mature, green trees and plants visible close to the entrance of the park at Barlett Cove in contrast to the bare, lunar-esque landscape closer to the terminus of the glaciers. This area has just recently been free of the weight of the glacier and has not had time to build life-sustaining soil.

On a good day, most ships are able to visit 3 to 4 tidewater glaciers. Sailing to the northwest, your visit may include the following: Mile 1 is Bartlett Cove, where your Rangers embark. The first glimpse of a tidewater glacier will probably be Mile 45, Reid Glacier, followed by Mile 46, Lamplugh Glacier. Both of these glaciers are flowing from the Brady Icefield which straddles the Fairweather Mountains. The tallest peak in the park is Mt. Fairweather (15,299 feet). The Fairweather and Wrangell-St. Elias Mountains combine to be the tallest coastal mountain range in the world. Continuing up Tarr Inlet, most ships stop to admire the Grand

Pacific Glacier at Mile 65. This glacier is one of the main tributaries that once filled the bay with ice. Today it is retreating very quickly; discussions are already underway as to how the park will be regulated when the terminus of the Grand Pacific retreats over the Canadian border. Also in Tarr Inlet is one of the most active tidewater glaciers in the park, Margerie Glacier at Mile 63. Due to the steep drop-off in front of the glacier, ships can be positioned amazingly close to the face. White Arctic terns and gulls nest in the rocks adjacent to the glacier; when the glacier calves it stuns krill and small fish, making it an ideal feeding spot for birds. During the spring, John Hopkins Inlet is prime habitat for female harbor seal and their pups. It is closed to ship traffic until late summer, when a limited number of ships are allowed to visit. Muir Glacier, named after John Muir, is an impressive tidewater glacier visited by smaller, expeditionary ships. Prior to 1860, Muir Glacier joined with Grand Pacific Glacier to form the huge glacial system that created the bay.

Though silted water is not the favored habitat for baleen whales, the more clear water at the mouth of the huge bay is one of the favorite feeding spots for humpback whales.

LANDMARKS AND POINTS OF INTEREST

CAPE SPENCER LIGHTHOUSE
Coordinates: 58° 13′ N, 136° 37′ W

Located in Cross Sound at the western entrance of Icy Strait, the manned lighthouse began service in 1925 and became automated in 1973.

FAIRWEATHER MOUNTAINS

Second tallest coastal mountain range in the world, the Fairweathers form the western boundary of Glacier Bay extending down to Icy Strait and out to the Pacific Coast as far north as Dry Bay.

GRAND PACIFIC GLACIER
Coordinates: 59° 05′ N, 137° 04′ W

Largest tidewater glacier in the Glacier Bay National Park, Grand Pacific is located at the northern reach of Tarr Inlet. Grand Pacific is the new generation remnant of the ancient glacier that once covered the entire bay. Pushing south when it was wider and deeper and longer, the glacier would have joined with the surrounding glaciers to cover the landscape with a thick sheet of moving ice.

ICY STRAIT

Coordinates: 8° 15′ N, 136° 26′ W (west entrance)

First charted by Captain James Cook in 1778, the strait begins at Cross Sound to the west and continues between Chichagof Island to the south and Glacier Bay National Park to the north and ends in the east at Chatham Strait. Cook named the entrance to the strait Cross Sound as it was discovered on Holy Cross Day. The name Icy Straits, however, comes from the Russian "ledenski" or icy, and was translated and thus named in 1852 by a local fishing captain.

JOHNS HOPKINS GLACIER

Coordinates: 58° 48′ N, 137° 08′ W

Tidewater glacier located on the western side of Glacier Bay, named for the Baltimore based university.

JOHNS HOPKINS INLET

Coordinates: 58° 54′ N, 136° 57′ W

Western branch of Glacier Bay, Johns Hopkins Inlet was named in 1893 for Johns Hopkins University. The inlet is one of the prime spots for harbor seals giving birth in the spring. Often the inlet is closed until late summer to protect new pups.

LAMPLUGH GLACIER

Coordinates: 58° 53′ N, 136° 54′ W

Tidewater glacier, located on the western side of Glacier Bay, was named for English geologist George Lamplugh, who visited the area in 1884.

MARGERIE GLACIER

Coordinates: 59° 02′ N, 137° 04′ W

Tidewater glacier located at the northwest end of Glacier Bay on Tarr Inlet, Margerie is perpendicular to Grand Pacific. The glacier was named after French geologist Emmanuel de Margerie who visited the area in 1913. Margerie is one of the most active glaciers in the park for calving.

MT. FAIRWEATHER

Elevation: 15,299 feet
Coordinates: 58° 54' N, 137° 31' W

Tallest peak within the Fairweather Range.

MUIR GLACIER

Coordinates: 59° 04' N, 136° 12' W

Tidewater glacier located up Muir Inlet, named after naturalist John Muir who visited the area in 1879.

POINT ADOLPHUS

Coordinates: 58° 17' N, 135° 46' W

Across Icy Straits from Gustavus is Point Adolphus. Located on the northeast corner of Chichagof Island, the point was named in 1794 by Captain George Vancouver for Aldolphus Frederick, son of King George III. In the summer, the sheltered water around Point Adolphus is a favorite area for humpback whales to feed. Good chance to see them if your ship detours to the area.

PORT FREDERICK

Coordinates: 58° 08' N, 135° 23' W

Inlet on the northeast edge of Chichagof Island, named in 1794 by Captain George Vancouver for Adolphus Frederick, son of King George III.

TARR INLET

Coordinates: 59° 03' N, 137° 02' W

Located at the northwestern branch of Glacier Bay, Tarr Inlet was named in 1912 for professor of geology Dr. Ralph Tarr.

139° 46' W

WRANGELL-SAINT ELIAS MOUNTAINS

CANADA

Mt. St. Elias
18,010 ft.

Mt. Augusta
14,070 ft.

Mt. Vancouver
15,700 ft.

Mt. Alverstone
14,500 ft.

Dome Pass

Mt. Cook
13,766 ft.

Mt. Seattle
10,399 ft.

Mt. Aylesworth
9,310 ft.

Mt. Herbert
6,090 ft.

Mt. Henry Clay
7,434 ft.

59° 32 N

Yakutat Bay
p. 196

Yakutat

FAIRWEATHER

Mt. Hay
8,870 ft.

Mt. Fairweather
15,300 ft.

MOUNTAINS

Glacier Bay

Gustavus

N
W   E
S

20 mi
50 km

PACIFIC OCEAN

139° 46' W

7 CRUISING YAKUTAT BAY

CITIES AND TOWNS

YAKUTAT

Coordinates: 59° 32′ N, 139° 46′ W
Population (2009):   580

Located on Monti Bay at the southeast mouth of Yakutat Bay, this small fishing community with its native roots was isolated until a 7,745 ft. airstrip was built during World War II. That airstrip is now the town's airport, which is serviced daily by Alaska Airlines. You can stroll along Cannon Beach and still see old WWII canon placements. Not far away is Harlequin Lake with its massive beached icebergs. Yakutat is world renowned for its excellent steelhead fishing in the Alsek and Situk Rivers. However, oddly enough, what most non-cruise tourists come to Yakutat for is surfing. The waves at Ocean Cape break as high as 6 feet, but you do need a good insulated wet suit!

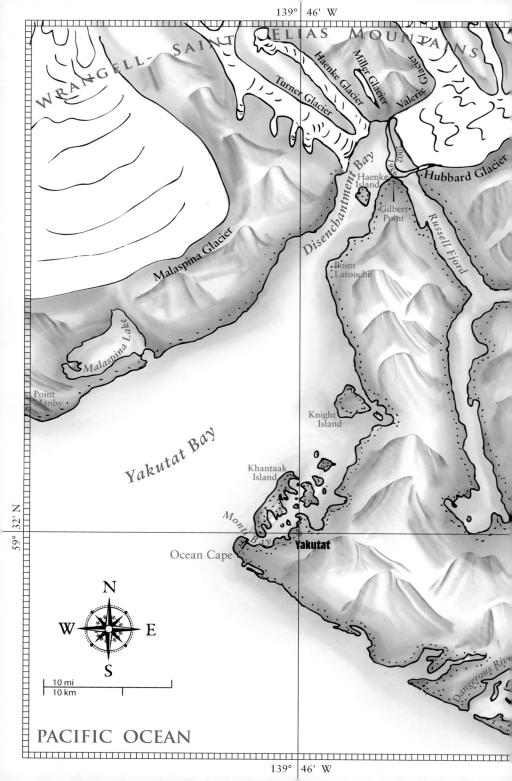

YAKUTAT BAY

Coordinates: 59° 40′ N, 139° 54′ W

Geographically and culturally, Yakutat Bay is considered the northern-most extent of Southeast Alaska. The name comes from the Tlingit word "Yak'taa t" which means "where the canoe rests." It was adulterated by Russian Yuri Lisianski who wrote it as Yakootat in 1805. However you spell it, Yakutat is a large, wide bay that owes its existence to the massive glacial system that once covered the coast. If you look at a map, you can see two glaciers, Hubbard and Malaspina. About 3,000 years ago both of these glaciers were longer and wider, extending out to what is now the Pacific coast, and merging together to form one huge sheet of ice. As Hubbard retreated the weight of the ice created a 23 mile wide by 26 mile long depression that became Yakutat Bay. For hundreds of years the ice stopped at the far northeast end of the bay. However, after another period of retreat, the glacier moved another 14 miles to the northeast, creating Disenchantment Bay. During this period of retreat, nearby Russell and Nuntak Fjords were also created. Back on the coast, Malaspina Glacier also shrunk in size, but unlike Hubbard--which was and is a tidewater glacier--Malaspina is a piedmont glacier, the largest in the world. Its source is up in the Wrangell-St. Elias Mountains but its terminus spreads out on dry land, covering the flatland at the valley floor. As we sail into Yakutat Bay the white glow you can see on the horizon on the port side is the Malaspina. Its area is about that of the country of Switzerland. However, because the majority of the glacier is at sea level it is very hard to see. If you are flying into or out of Anchorage, on a clear day you can see Malaspina easily from the air.

Nowhere on earth will you see more spectacular mountains from the sea than the Wrangell-St. Elias Mountains – the world's tallest coastal mountain range. Facing Yakutat Bay, on the port side, to the northwest, is the pyramidal peak, Mt. St. Elias. At 18,010 feet above sea level, it is 75 miles from the coast. To the southeast, on the starboard side, is Mt. Fairweather; at 15,299 feet it is the tallest peak within the Fairweather Range. Given the disproportionately large size of these mountains, scale and perspective is distorted. To give you a sense of comparison, most ships are dwarfed by the glacier.

According to the ancestors of the Yakutat Tlingits, Mt. St. Elias is the husband of Mt. Fairweather and all the peaks in between are their children.

The first European mariner to identify the bay was Vitus Bering in 1741. In 1778, Captain James Cook spotted what he thought to be Bering's Mt. St. Elias; if so, then the bay he entered in May of that year probably was Yakutat. In 1786, La Perouse named the entire bay Baie de Monti or Monti Bay after the second in command of his ship, the Astrolabe. The small cove in front of the town of Yakutat still bears his name. The same year British Captain Nathaniel Potlock also entered and named the bay Admiralty. But it wasn't until 1791 that the Italian mariner Alessandro Malaspina, searching for the Northwest Passage on behalf of Spain, fully explored the bay and its upper reaches. Hoping to find the Northwest Passage, he was saddened to see that a huge wall of ice prevented him from continuing further. He named the bay "Disenchantment."

FACTS

198

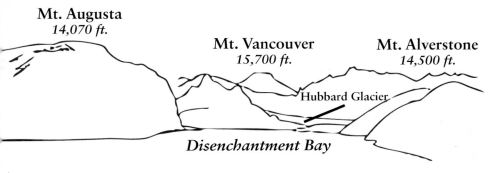

Mt. Augusta
14,070 ft.

Mt. Vancouver
15,700 ft.

Mt. Alverstone
14,500 ft.

Hubbard Glacier

Disenchantment Bay

At Mile 1 at the mouth of Yakutat Bay, southbound ships will stop to board the required Southeast Alaskan pilots. At the same time, some cruise lines also host a group of Tlingits from the town of Yakutat. They provide the Native American perspective on this, their traditional land. Upon leaving the bay, the ship will stop in the same place to disembark the Tlingit guests. On trips continuing north, the Southeast Pilots will also hop off.

Once inside, it takes approximately 2½ hours to cross the bay. You may start to see ice built up on the far northern edge of the bay to the port side. The current coming from Disenchantment Bay flows to the north, carrying ice out to sea in this direction. However, occasionally ice will build up in both Yakutat and Disenchantment Bays, slowing down your ship's speed. Everything is dependent on ice conditions in areas of tidewater glaciers. The captain must proceed with caution to avoid ice damage to the ship's propellers.

The story of the Alaska Panhandle.

In 1825, Russia and Great Britain came to an agreement regarding the interpretation of who owned what in North America. Russia's main interest was to have coastal access as far south as possible for the trapping of sea otters. According to the 1825 agreement, Russian territory began north of 54° 40' and extended to the west of the summits of the coastal range until the boundary reached the 141° parallel, where it would run due north to the Arctic Ocean. When the United States purchased Alaska in 1867, they wanted the border clarified. The Canadians believed that the measurement of 30 miles from the sea inland began at the mouth of all the bays and inlets to the corresponding peaks. The United States argued that it was 30 miles from the head of all the bays and inlets, as the Russians would have never settled for 30 miles from the mouth because that would have denied them hundreds of miles of valuable coastline. In the International Boundary Commission of 1895, the line was drawn according to the United States proposal of 30 miles from the head of all the bays and inlets to the highest corresponding peaks thus creating

the panhandle. Take a good look at a map of this area and you can see the boundary peaks. When the boundary reached 141° W, at Mt. St. Elias – the tallest peak of the coastal range – the line runs due north.

Even at a distance of almost thirty miles, you can see Hubbard Glacier at the far end of the bay. To see something so clearly at such a distance, it has to be BIG! Hubbard is the largest tidewater glacier in the world. It is 6 miles wide, 1200 feet deep and 76 miles long. The face is 200–400 feet tall! To give you a sense of comparison most ships are about 140 feet tall. Gazing at the face of the glacier with nothing but nature around, it all looks very manageable. However, if another cruise ship is visiting at the same time, you will be amazed at how that huge ship looks like a bathtub toy in front of Hubbard Glacier!

Yakutat Bay narrows as you pass Point Latouche, Mile 26, which is the official entrance to Disenchantment Bay. Off the starboard bow is Haenke Island, Mile 34. The Tlingits call it Egg Island as it previously was used to collect sea gull eggs. Straight ahead is Hubbard Glacier, Mile 36. To the left, perpendicular to Hubbard, is a series of three glaciers that merge into one rather black looking terminus; they are Haenke, Turner and Miller Glaciers. Miller Glacier, located at the far right closest to Hubbard, can hardly be called a glacier. It is covered by a thick terminal moraine. Underneath it continues to melt and thin, dropping the moraine, filling the valley beneath. Turner and Haenke Glaciers are tidewater and do calve, though the star of this show is, by far, Hubbard.

From your ship, Hubbard may not look like it is 6 miles wide. The reason is, what you see is not what you get. What you see from the ship is only one half of the glacier's face. The rest curves around behind Gilbert Point, Mile 35, into Russell Fjord. Gilbert Point is the point of land to the starboard bow where Hubbard ends on the right. In fact, if you were able to fly over Gilbert Point you would see that the glacier wraps around for another 3 miles to the southeast. It was at Gilbert Point that in 1986, after an unprecedented surge, Hubbard moved at a rate of over 100 feet a day pushing ice against Gilbert Point, damming off Russell Fjord. A similar episode happened again in 2002.

Though Hubbard is substantially larger than any other glacier in the state, its icebergs are relatively small for its great size. Hubbard is one of the few glaciers that continues to advance or grow in size. The amount of snow falling up in the Wrangell-St. Elias Mountains produces so much ice that the glacier is being pushed along at a rate of about 3- 5 feet day. The gradual slope of the terrain over which it travels allows it to move unimpeded, without compacting or regelating (re-freezing). Unlike South Sawyer Glacier in Tracy Arm--that is small and short but very compressed, producing huge icebergs relative to its size--Hubbard expels thousands of tons of shattered ice. The great icebergs of Titanic fame are calved from sheets of continental ice thousands of feet thick. Lucky for cruise ships, no continental ice exists along your Southeast Alaska itinerary. Considering its enormous size, glaciologists at the University of Alaska/Fairbanks estimate the ice at the terminus of Hubbard glacier to be only between 700 - 1,000 years old.

202

LANDMARKS AND POINTS OF INTEREST

DISENCHANTMENT BAY
Coordinates: 59° 58′ N, 139° 32′ W

The northeastern arm of Yakutat Bay, discovered by Captain Alessandro Malaspina in 1791. Malaspina was searching for the Northwest Passage and was disappointed that this promising inlet was a dead end-- therefore the name, "Disenchantment." From its entrance at Point Latouche to the face of Hubbard Glacier, the bay measures approximately 6 miles.

GILBERT POINT
Coordinates: 59° 59′ N, 139° 28′ W

Point of land on the northeast end of Disenchantment Bay; bisects Hubbard Glacier at its mid-section. Gilbert Point is the land that separates Disenchantment Bay from Russell Fjord and is where Hubbard Glacier built up a wall of ice during the surge of 1987 and 2002. It was named by Prof. Ralph Tarr in honor of Grove Karl Gilbert, who served from 1889-1892 as the first chief geologist of the United States Geological Survey.

HAENKE ISLAND
Coordinates: 59° 59′ N, 139° 30 W

Island located at the head of Disenchantment Bay. Named after biologist Tadeo Haencke who sailed with Captain Alessandro Malaspina. The Yakutat Tlingits know the island as Egg Island, for its availability of seagull eggs.

HUBBARD GLACIER
Coordinates: 60° 03′ N, 139° 27′ W

Largest, single, tidewater glacier in the world, named in 1890 for Gardiner G. Hubbard, regent of the Smithsonian Institute and founder of The National Geographic Society. Hubbard Glacier is 76 miles long, 6 miles wide, and approximately 1200 feet deep, with a towering 400 foot wall of exposed ice at the face.

MALASPINA GLACIER

Coordinates: 59° 52′ N, 140° 32′ W

Located at the foot of the Wrangell-St. Elias Mountains, the vast flat area of white to the northwest of Yakutat Bay is the Malaspina Glacier. Named after explorer Alessandro Malaspina, the glacier is the largest piedmont glacier in North America, measuring 60 miles in length, with a thickness of approximately 1,200 feet.

MT. ST. ELIAS

Elevation: 18,010 feet
Coordinates: 60° 18′ N, 140° 56 W

Tallest peak of the Wrangell-St. Elias Mountains and the point at which the border between Alaska and Canada runs straight north to the arctic. Named in 1791, by Vitus Bering, who first spotted the peak as it came through the clearing fog on the Danish day of St. Elias.

POINT LATOUCHE

Coordinates: 59° 53′ N, 139° 37′ W

Located in the northeast of Yakutat Bay, it marks the beginning of Disenchantment Bay. Named by Captain George Vancouver for William Digges Latouche who married Mary Grace Puget, the sister of Vancouver's lieutenant Peter Puget.

RUSSELL FJORD

Coordinates: 59° 51′ N, 139° 30′ W

Russell Fjord is a glacially created body of water extending 31 miles to the southeast of Gilbert Point. Water from Russell Fjord flows out to the sea by way of the narrow passage in front of Hubbard Glacier at Gilbert Point. It was Russell Fjord that was dammed when Hubbard Glacier surged in 1986 and 2002, causing melt water to rise threatening to flood downstream communities. The fjord was named after Israel Russell, a geologist who first explored the bay.

TURNER/HAENKE, MILLER GLACIERS

Coordinates: 60° 03 N, 139° 35′ W

Complex of tidewater glaciers flowing into Disenchantment Bay from
their source in the Wrangell-St. Elias Mountains. Haenke Glacier was
named after biologist Tadeo Haencke; Turner Glacier for geologist John
Henry Turner of the US Coastal & Geodetic Survey. Turner and Haenke
glaciers are 21 miles in length and 3.7 miles wide at the terminus. Miller
Glacier, located to the right, is covered by a terminal moraine. Most of the
glacier underneath has melted away, causing glaciologists to speculate it
no longer exists.

WRANGELL-ST. ELIAS MOUNTAINS

The Wrangell-St. St. Elias Mountains form the coastal spine of Southeast
Alaska. Along with the Fairweather Range, they are the tallest coastal
mountains in the world.

Why do we need pilots?

Fear not, the Captain knows what
he is doing. Cruise ships sailing in
the coastal waterways of Alaska
are required to carry two pilots.
It is the responsibility of the pilot
to ensure the safe navigation of
the ship through the myriad of
channels and straits of South-
east Alaska. The pilots are seasoned veterans who know the
proclivity of the area, the tide, current, wind, and traffic. They
confer with the Captain and his officers, giving input regarding the proposed course. They are also onboard to ensure that
traffic safety and environmental regulations are followed.

FACTS

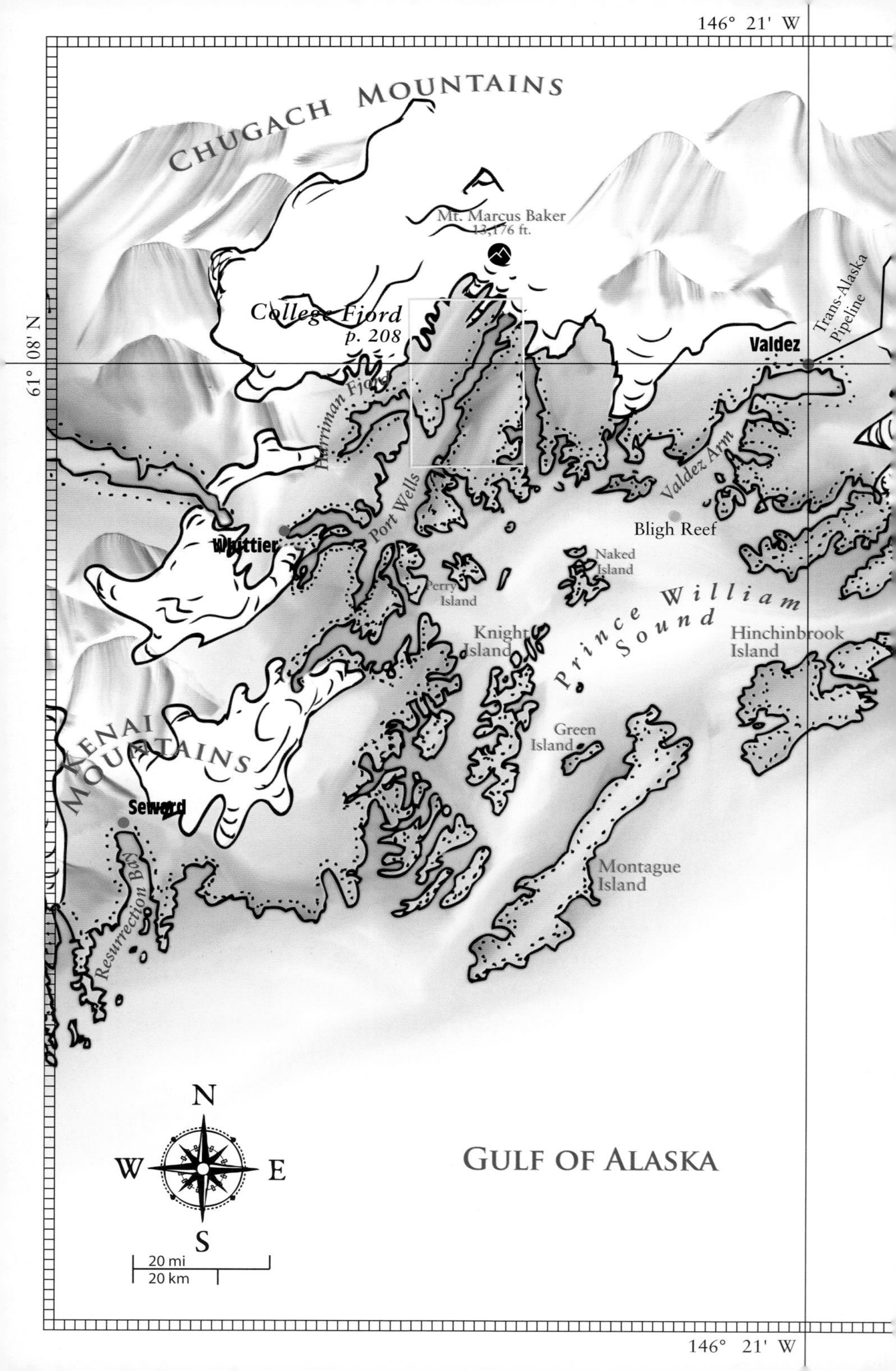

CHUGACH MOUNTAINS

Mt. Marcus Baker
13,176 ft.

College Fiord
p. 208

Harriman Fiord

Valdez

Trans-Alaska
Pipeline

61° 08' N

Port Wells

Valdez Arm

Whittier

Bligh Reef

Naked
Island

Perry
Island

Prince William
Sound

Knight
Island

Hinchinbrook
Island

KENAI
MOUNTAINS

Green
Island

Seward

Montague
Island

Resurrection Bay

N

W   E

S

GULF OF ALASKA

20 mi
20 km

CRUISING
PRINCE WILLIAM SOUND

CITIES AND TOWNS

VALDEZ

Coordinates: 61° 08' N, 146° 21' W
Population (2005):   4,020

The town of Valdez is located at the far northeast corner of Prince William Sound at the head of Valdez Arm. It was named by Spanish Captain Don Salvador Fidalgo in 1790 in honor of Spanish naval officer Admiral Antonio Valdez y Basan. Valdez was destroyed by tsunami after the 1984 Good Friday earthquake. Today Valdez it is the terminus of the Trans Alaska Pipeline. Visitors can drive to Valdez by way of the Richardson Highway.

SCENIC SAILING

COLLEGE FJORD

Coordinates: 61° 08' N, 147° 52' W (mouth)
Coordinates: 61° 16' N, 147° 43' W (northernmost)

It is no wonder Edward Harriman decided on this waterway for his geologic expedition. It contains not only the greatest concentration of tidewater glaciers in any one body of water in Alaska but also the most fascinating glaciers. It is an open air laboratory of natural science.

Technically located in Southcentral Alaska, College Fjord is an estuary of Prince William Sound tucked up in the northeast end of Port Wells, making it the northernmost point for most cruise ships. It is 25 miles long and 3 miles wide and contains 18 glaciers, 7 of which are tidewater, which is the greatest concentration of glaciers of any single body of water in the state.

In 1899, Edward Harriman, the industrialist of railroad fame, sponsored a geologic expedition to study glaciers. Onboard he invited 30 geologists plus the photographer Edward Curtis. Each geologist dedicated himself to

207

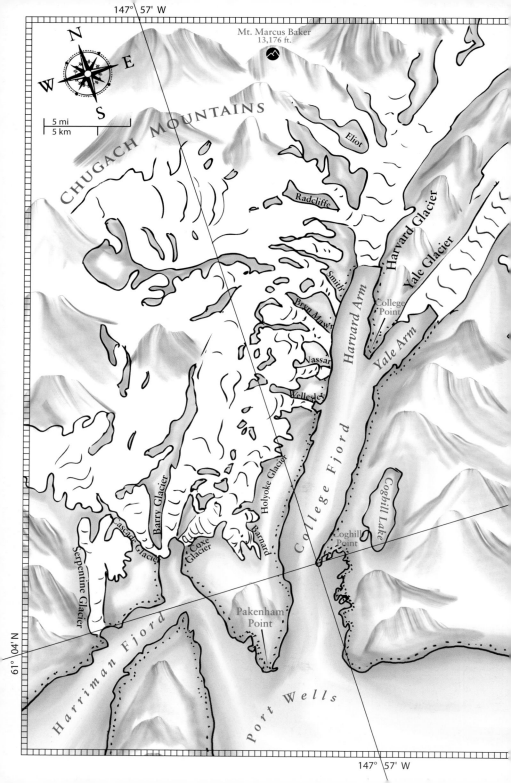

the study of one glacier which was later named in honor of a university. That is why many glaciers around Prince William Sound have a collegiate ring; Columbia, Harvard, Yale, etc. were all named during the Harriman Expedition. This tradition continued until 1908, when Muir Glacier, located in what is now Glacier Bay National Park, was named after John Muir. In 1910, Lawrence Martin, who was then the head of the National Geographic Society, named Eliot and Lowell Glaciers after former Harvard presidents who were also generous National Geographic supporters.

Like most fjords, College Fjord is exceptionally deep, averaging 900 feet. About two thousand years ago all the glaciers you see today were deeper and wider, merging together to fill the entire valley with one massive sheet of ice. Today the remaining 18 glaciers, including the 7 tidewater glaciers, are evidence of this ancient history. The two largest glaciers within this system are located at the far end of the fjord, with Harvard Glacier on the left and Yale on the right. Of the two, Harvard is larger. The other tidewater glaciers include Smith, Bryn Mawr, Vassar and Wellesley. Non-tidewater glaciers are Barnard, Holyoke, Radcliffe, Amherst, Dartmouth, Lafayette, Baltimore, Eliot, Lowell, and Crescent (which was named for its shape.)

The north of Prince William Sound is ringed by the Chugach Mountains. It is from this high range that snow accumulates to feed the many glaciers in this area. On a clear day Mt. Marcus Baker, at 13,176 feet the tallest peak of the range, will be visible at the head of College Fjord.

Sea otters float on their backs, allowing the current to carry them into the mouth of College Fjord. In the early summer you will see females with furry little lumps on their chests; look closely because each lump is actually a new pup.

Notice the patch of dead trees on both the port and starboard sides of the ship as you enter; these trees died during the tsunami that hit this part of Port William Sound after the 1984 earthquake, Mile 3.

Most of the glaciers in College Fjord are located on the western side of the fjord or the port side, as you enter. The first two are Holyoke and Barnard at Mile 12; both are hanging glaciers suspended above the valley floor. The first tidewater is Wellesley at Mile 15; followed by Vassar at Mile 17. Vassar is a classic example of a tidewater glacier with a well- developed terminal moraine. Notice that the two glaciers on either side of Vassar are clean in color and end vertically in the sea. Vassar has a brown terminus that stretches out into the fjord. The terminal moraine acts as a blanket, insulating the glacier and preventing it from calving and melting. So it is growing, pushing out into the fjord under the moraine However, one day when the glacier stops receiving the snow necessary to turn to ice to feed it, the terminus will start to thin and melt back, leaving the moraine with no support. Gradually the terminal moraine will drop into the sea and form either an extension of the land or an island. Long Island, New York for example, is a terminal moraine. Use your binoculars to look closely at the growth on the moraine; what looks like moss and scrub from a distance is actually mature 40-foot trees. When moraine first forms it is sterile, ground rock. It takes a long time for it to develop into soil rich and deep enough to support any growth, let alone a huge tree. So you know, this has been there for a long time.

Bryn Mawr, Mile 18 ½, is another textbook example of glaciology. Here you have two branches of the glacier joining together uphill like merg- ing lanes on a freeway. As they meet the lateral moraine, ice from each is squeezed together to form one clean medial moraine down the center of the terminus. You can see the plastic nature of the glacial ice as it bends and stretches around the outcropping of rock called a nunatak.

Smith Glacier at Mile 20 and Baltimore Glacier, Mile 21, are the last glaciers not flowing into Harvard. Straight ahead is Harvard Glacier at Mile 23, the largest in the fjord. It is 3 miles wide and about 47 miles long. Radcliffe, Eliot, Lowell and Donner are all tributaries following into Harvard. Harvard Glacier is advancing, unlike nearby Yale, Mile 21. While you view Harvard Glacier you cannot see Yale. It is hidden by College Point Mile 18, which is the point of land at the end of the Dora Keen range that separates the two glaciers. Watch for Yale as you sail up the fjord or on your return. Yale is retreating. It has retreated back 4 miles in the last ten years. It is also 3 miles wide but only 32 miles in length.

For those of you on the starboard side, remember all the great views will be coming up on your side as you head back into Prince William Sound. Don't forget the otters.

LANDMARKS AND POINTS OF INTEREST

BARRY GLACIER

Coordinates: 61° 07′ N, 148° 06′ W

Approximately 15 miles in length, Barry Glacier is a tidewater glacier flowing into Harriman Fjord. Named for geologist William Barry.

BLIGH REEF - SITE OF THE EXXON VALDEZ DISASTER

Coordinates: 60° 50′ N, 146° 54′ W

Located at the southern end of Valdez Arm in Prince William Sound, Bligh reef was named by Captain James Cook in honor of William Bligh, who later went on to HMS Bounty fame. It was on Bligh Reef, in 1987, that the Exxon Valdez went aground, spilling 13 million gallons of crude oil throughout the sound.

CHUGACH MOUNTAINS

The mountain range that arcs over the northern ridge of Prince William Sound. Tallest peak in the Chugach Range is Mt. Marcus Baker (13,176 feet). Snow collected by the Chugach Mountains feeds the glaciers of College Fjord.

COGHILL POINT
Coordinates: 61° 04' N, 147° 57' W

The point of land at the southeast entrance of College Fjord. Notice the dead trees on both sides of the fjord; these are trees that died as the result of the 1964 tsunami following the Good Friday earthquake in Anchorage.

COLLEGE POINT
Coordinates: 61° 12' N, 147° 45' W

The point of land that separates Harvard Glacier from Yale Glacier at the head of College Fjord. Facing Harvard Glacier (north), College Point is on the starboard side.

HARRIMAN FJORD
Coordinates: 61° 04' N, 148° 14' W

Northeast section of Prince William Sound, located at the end of Port Wells and the mouth of College Fjord. Harriman Fjord is accessible only to smaller expeditionary ships. Named and explored in 1899, by the Edward Harriman Expedition.

MOUNT MARCUS BAKER

| Elevation: | 13,176 feet |
| Coordinates: | 61° 26′ N, 147° 45′ W |

Tallest peak visible from College Fjord; tallest peak of the Chugach Mountain Range. Named in 1879 for Marcus Baker, who served with the Coast Survey and Geologic Survey of Alaska and was the author of the 1906 book, Geographic Dictionary of Alaska.

PORT WELLS

Coordinates: 60° 51′ N, 148° 13′ W

Body of water in northeast Prince William Sound between Ester Island and the mainland. Named by Captain George Vancouver after John Wells who married Ester Puget, sister of Peter Puget. Port Wells is the gateway to College Fjord.

PRINCE WILLIAM SOUND

Coordinates: 60° 28′ N, 147° 37′ W

Located in the northeast extent of the Gulf of Alaska, Prince William Sound has the greatest concentration of tidewater glaciers, more than any other region in the state. There are 40 glaciated fjords that drain into the Sound, with 20 tidewater glaciers. It was named in 1794 by Captain George Vancouver for Prince William, third child and third son of King George III who later became King William IV. In 1778, Captain Cook was the first European to sail Prince William Sound; however, in honor of his patron the Earl of Sandwich, he named it Sandwich Sound.

CITIES AND TOWNS

WHITTIER

Coordinates:	60° 46′ N, 148° 41′ W
Population (2009):	163

Whittier's history may be more interesting than the town. Located at the head of Prince William Sound prior to World War II, not much was there. The main track of the Alaskan Railroad went from Anchorage to Seward, 126 miles away. Though the inlet at the head of Passage Canal was 55 miles away from Anchorage, mountains kept the area isolated. Seizing an opportunity, the military decided to blast a tunnel through to the hidden bay and build a spur off the track to this closer, ice-free port. Military goods and provisions were transported more expeditiously to Anchorage, and the remote, secret location of the port made it perfect for storing sensitive material, including fuel. The town of Whittier was born.

After the war, the town pretty much closed up. Then in 1948, the barrack-like Begich Building was constructed, becoming the main housing complex and community hub. A tunnel was later built between the building and the elementary school. But there wasn't much there other than a bar and a bait shop.

The Tunnel

Alaska State Department of Transportation says:

- Longest highway tunnel in North America at 2.5 miles.

- Longest combined rail and highway use tunnel in North America.

- First U.S. tunnel with jet turbine and portal fan ventilation.

- First computerized regulation of both rail and highway traffic.

- First tunnel designed for -40° F. and 150 mph winds.

- Portal buildings designed to withstand avalanches.

One of the reasons the town never grew was its isolation. The only way you could get to Whittier was by train. Vehicles were loaded onto the train cars and transported into the community from the highway. In the early years of Alaskan cruising, when Whittier was first used as a cruise terminus, passengers had to board buses that drove up onto railroad cars that then transported them in or out of town.

Today the tunnel has been updated. The Anton Anderson Memorial Tunnel is now paved for cars, but still accommodates trains. In the summer of 2009, Whittier had 40 stops by cruise ships. Buses can now make the shorter drive to Whittier from Anchorage;   drivers, however, must time their entry into the town to coincide with when the tunnel is open for traffic. The railway tunnel, the only way in to town, is open fifteen minutes for northbound traffic and fifteen minutes for southbound traffic every hour. The rest of the hour is held for the train!

Not only is Whittier being used by cruise ships, but local fisherman and boaters from Anchorage are coming down. In response to the increase in visitors, a new hotel has been constructed, along with several storefronts for tour operators, fishing charter companies, restaurants and souvenir shops. The port is not chosen for its intrinsic interest but rather for its proximity to Anchorage. You'll enjoy the ride past Portage Glacier and Turnagain Arm on your way to or from Anchorage. And if you are boarding your ship in Whittier, the glaciers that line Passage Canal provide a breathtaking start to a spectacular cruise.

SEWARD

Coordinates:	60° 07′ N, 149° 26′ W
Population (2005):	3,126

Seward is a delightful town that is known as the Gateway to the Kenai. Set against a backdrop of the Kenai Mountains, Seward is located on Resurrection Bay, 126 miles from Anchorage. Named after Secretary of State William Seward, the town was founded in 1903. The weight of glaciers and the wear of rivers carved out a natural depression across the Kenai Peninsula from Anchorage south to Seward. The mail run, railroad, and later the highway followed this natural open path. Seward became the closest port to Anchorage for vessels not wishing to sail around Cook Inlet. In 1903, the Alaska Central Railway linked Anchorage to the ice free port of Seward. Now the Seward Highway National Scenic Byway follows the same route, hugging the coast, then winding through breathtaking mountain passes. There still is train service; during the summer The Alaska Railroad Coastal Classic runs between the two towns. Guests embarking or disembarking in Seward take either the highway or rail.

It was following this same path in 1925, that diphtheria serum was transported from Seward to Nenana by train and then north to Nome by dog sled in what later became the famous Iditarod Race. Long before the train, the trail was used to transport mail and goods from Seward to the gold miners in places like Hope and Sunrise. When diphtheria broke out in far away Nome the fastest way to get the serum to the ice bound village was by dog sled. Today the 1,049 mile race is run from Wasilla to Nome. The world's record for fastest time is currently held by Martin Buser who in 2002 completed the race in 8 days, 22 hours, 46 minutes, and 2 seconds.

Mt. Marathon dominates the town. Like a mother cradling her child, the 3,022 foot tall mountain hovers over Seward. Mt. Marathon is the site of the Independence Run – yes run. Runners from around the world compete to see who will have the best time running up and down the shale covered peak. There are categories for men, women, children and seniors. In 2009, 400 runners competed. The best time is 43 minutes 39 sec.!

Seward is the Gateway to the Kenai National Park. It is a 15 minute drive to Exit Glacier, 7 miles north of town. There are trails for all abilities that will bring you right up to the terminus of the glacier. It is even wheelchair accessible to the small visitor's center, far enough to see the glacier. Ranger station and restrooms are on site. Regular shuttles as well as taxis operate from Seward. It is not recommended to walk from town as the road from the highway is unpaved. For the serious hiker, trails lead up to the Harding Icefield.

Those of you with some time for exploring may want to take the trolley into town or walk the 1.5 miles. From your ship you can see that Seward is divided into two sections; the new part of town around the small boat harbor was built within the last twenty years, and the old part of town is what is left after the 1964, 9.2 magnitude Good Friday earthquake. Seward felt the quake that hit in nearby Anchorage, but the town was destroyed by the ensuing tsunami. Twelve people died from the tsunami; 131 people in total died as a result of the quake. Eighty-six homes were destroyed and Seward's commercial and economic base was shattered. To learn what happened and see how Seward was affected, stop by the earthquake exhibit at the Seward Museum. While there take a look around at some of the town's artifacts dating back to the time of the old Russian shipyard and the pioneering Lowell family.

The Alaska SeaLife Center is located at 301 Railway Avenue. This new, state-of-the-art, non-profit marine science facility has excellent exhibits of local marine life including puffin dive ponds, seal pools and interactive tanks where you can touch sea urchins and baby octopi. One of the primary purposes of the Center is to study reasons for the decline in marine populations and to figure out how they can be rehabilitated. To that end, there is an excellent exhibit explaining the Valdez oil spill. Some ongoing research projects are also open to the public. The SeaLife Center is wheelchair accessible. After this introduction to the ecosystems of the area, those interested in getting up close and personal with the marine life of Resurrection Bay can book an excursion through the Kenai fjords with any number of local companies.

Seward is known for its great fishing and every summer fisherman flock to the town for the Silver Salmon Derby. Tagged fish can bring in prize money of up to $100,000. In 2002, the record was set by Shirley Baysinger who caught a 22.24 pound silver.

Local treat:

Everyone has their favorite place for Alaska's famous halibut fish 'n chips. Mine is The Marina. Located across from the small boat harbor, the chunks of pan-fried halibut are huge and juicy. The fish is doused in flour, not dipped in batter. It is light, not greasy, and fresh, fresh, fresh! (We all miss you dearly, Judy.)

TIPS

With so much beauty surrounding Seward, it's not surprising that local artists have been inspired to express themselves. In addition to shops and galleries featuring local artists, some of that inspiration is displayed on the many murals painted around town. Artists are encouraged to adorn the buildings throughout town. There are five beautiful murals that depict everything from Seward's history to its wildflowers.

SCENIC SITES

BENNY BENSON MEMORIAL

Off the Seward Highway just a short walk from the Small Boat Harbor is the monument to Benny Benson, the young boy with the grand vision of Alaska. Benny Benson, the 13 year old Alaskan Native, was the winner of the territorial flag contest. Benny won the contest and his famous design now flies as the state flag. The flag was first flown in Seward, where Benny lived at the Jesse Lee Home. You can read about Benny and then enjoy the nature walk along the nearby lake.

EXIT GLACIER

Coordinates: 60° 08' N, 149° 24' W

Up close and personal with a glacier, visitors can explore several well marked trails that will take you right up to Exit Glacier. Flowing from the Harding Icefield, Exit Glacier is 3 miles long. Over the past hundred years its retreat has been studied by glaciologists and it is clearly marked within the park. Harding Icefield is 3.5 miles away on a trail accessible only during daylight hours. The first quarter mile of the trail is paved and wheelchair accessible. Take Mile 3 exit off the Seward Highway.

MARATHON MOUNTAIN

Elevation: 3,022 feet

Part of the Kenai Mountains, Mt. Marathon provides the dramatic back-drop to the town of Seward. The Mt. Marathon Independence Day Run is every July 4th. Runners from all around the world vie to see who can make it up and down the mountain in the best time. The top of the peak is above the tree line with slippery exposed shale that makes the run very difficult and dangerous for the amateur.

PORTAGE GLACIER

Coordinates: 60° 48' N, 148° 45' W

Located just 11 miles from the town of Whittier off the Seward Highway, Portage Glacier is the most accessible and most studied glacier in the state. From the visitors center you can see the extent of the glacier's retreat. Now approximately seven miles in length, Portage Lake was created by melt water.

LANDMARKS AND POINTS OF INTEREST

BEAR GLACIER

Coordinates: 59° 51' N, 149° 24' W

Located on the southwest mouth of Resurrection Bay, catch a glimpse of Bear Glacier from the ship's stern, on the starboard side. The glacier is large, about 10 miles in length, and flows from the Harding Icefield within the Kenai National Park.

BLACKSTONE GLACIER

Coordinates: 60° 38' N, 148° 43' W

Named in 1899 by W.C. Mendenhall of the United States Geologic Survey for a miner who lost his life in the area during the winter of 1896.

HARDING ICEFIELD

The Harding Icefield is the largest icefield contained within the United States. It covers over 300 square miles, feeds over 40 glaciers, and takes up half of the entire 607,805 acres of the Kenai National Park. The icefield is named after President Warren G. Harding, first United States president to visit the territory of Alaska.

KENAI FJORDS NATIONAL PARK

Established as a national park in 1978, Kenai Fjords is a spectacular combination of mountains, glaciers and maritime wildlife. Tours are available from the visitor's center in Seward as well as many local tour operators. Exit Glacier, also part of the park, is a fifteen minute taxi ride from town.

PASSAGE CANAL
Coordinates: 60° 48′ N, 148° 26′ W

Northwest corner of Prince William Sound, Passage Canal is west of Wells Passage and Port Wells, at the entrance to College Fjord. The town of Whittier is located at the head of Passage Canal. Named by Captain George Vancouver, the waterway provided passage to Turnagain Arm at the head of Cook Inlet.

RESURRECTION BAY
Coordinates: 59° 57' N, 149° 23' W

Resurrection Bay runs north and south and empties into Blying Sound at the northwest portion of the Gulf of Alaska. The bay was first explored by Russian Alesander Baranof in 1794, and named upon his departure on Easter Sunday. According to Sail Magazine, Resurrection Bay is one of America's top 10 greatest places to sail owing to its southerly winds that blow daily during the summer.

SUNNY COVE STATE MARINE PARK
Coordinates: 59° 51' N, 149° 24' W

Southeast mouth of Resurrection Bay on El Dorado Narrows, Sunny Cove State Marine Park contains interesting islands carved into arch-like formations. If you just embarked in Seward and are sailing southbound, take a few minutes about one hour after departure to watch for puffins flying from their nests along the craggy walls of the island's cliffs. The beaches are popular with sea lions. Hive Island is known for its military fortification. The walls of the now defunct building look like the ruins of a medieval castle.

TEBENKOFF GLACIER
Coordinates: 60° 43' N, 148° 28' W

Named in 1879 by W.H. Dall for Captain Michael Dmitrierich Tebenkov, governor of the Russian-American colonies from 1845-1850. Captain Tebenkov is known for his comprehensive Atlas of the NW Coast of America. The glacier measures 8 miles in length.

WHITTIER GLACIER
Coordinates: 60° 46' N, 148° 43' W

Named in 1915 for the poet John Greenleaf Whittier (1807-1892).

TERRY'S CRUISE POSTSCRIPT

PART 3

1 TERRY'S POSTSCRIPT
TASTE OF ALASKA

RECIPES BY EXECUTIVE CHEF MIKE RÖMHILD

Wishing to capture the taste of Alaska, Executive Chef Mike Römhild (www.chefmikeroemhild.com) seeks out local recipes and fresh local ingredients to create delicious Alaskan inspired dishes onboard the most prestigious cruise ships in the world. After years of scouring markets and frequenting fishing docks, he has put together a selection of his own Alaskan recipes that he generously shares with us here. Hopefully during your cruise you will have an opportunity to sample some of the local specialties. And when you return home you can try some of Chef Mike's Alaskan favorites.

CLASSIC ALASKAN SALMON SPREAD

INGREDIENTS:

- 5 ounces of hot smoked salmon
- 1 package of cream cheese
- 2 tbsp. sour cream
- 2 tbsp. lemon juice
- 1 tbsp. mild horseradish
- 1 tbsp. chives
- Salt and pepper to taste

PREPARATION:

Mix all ingredients to smooth paste. Can use a food processor for a more mousse-like consistency. Serve with crackers.

TARTAR OF ALASKAN SALMON

INGREDIENTS:

- 4 tbsp Alaskan salmon fillet, finely diced
- 2 tbsp steamed sushi rice
- 2 tbsp avocado, diced
- ½ tbsp finely chopped parsley
- 20 piece black grapes, peeled, quartered and seeded
- grated zest of ½ lemon
- little salt to taste
- 1 tsp soy sauce
- 1 tsp fresh lemon juice
- 2 tbsp salmon roe
- 2 tbsp wasabi mayonnaise
- 4 sprigs chervil
- 2 tbsp arugula lemon oil to garnish

PREPARATION:

- In a bowl mix together the salmon, rice, avocado, parsley, grapes and lemon zest.
- Add the salmon roe and wasabi mayonnaise.
- Divide between 4 serving plates and garnish each with a sprig of chervil before serving.

ALASKAN SALMON DUET

INGREDIENTS:

- 2 oz Alaskan Salmon Fillet, skinned
- 1 oz hot smoked Alaskan Salmon
- ½ tsp. capers
- ½ tsp. chopped fresh chervil
- Extra virgin olive oil,
- Lime juice, salt and pepper to taste
- 1 tbsp. sour cream
- Chopped chives, chervil, parsley
- 1 sprig chervil

PREPARATION:

- Flake the hot smoked salmon with a fork. Add chopped herbs, sour cream and a bit of pepper. Mix well to the consistency of an spread.
- Cut the fresh salmon fillet in very fine pieces, place in a kitchen bowl, add the capers, chervil, salt and pepper, olive oil and lime juice to taste and mix carefully.
- To assemble, use a ring mold (can use a clean tuna can with top and bottom removed.)
- Place the fresh tuna tartar in the mold and top with the smoked salmon spread.
- Garnish with the chervil sprig.

233

CHAR GRILLED KING ALASKAN SALMON

INGREDIENTS:

- 4 portions of Alaska King salmon
- 1 cup clarified butter
- Lemon juice from half a lemon
- Chopped dill, tarragon, chives, parsley
- Season to taste: Tabasco, Worcestershire sauce, crushed black pepper

PREPARATION:

- Mix butter with all ingredients and keep warm. Start grilling the salmon without any seasoning.
- Brush butter mixture on the fillet as you grill on both sides. Grill to preferred temperatures (Chef's recommendation is medium)
- Brush again with butter before serving. Garnish with lemon wedge.
- Serving suggestion: Honey mustard, European style cocktail sauce, cherry tomato salsa, or dill crème fraise.

ALASKAN SALMON BURGER

WITH TOMATO CHIVE CRÈME FRAICHE - SERVES 4

INGREDIENTS:

Burger:
- 1 ½ pound fresh Alaskan salmon fillet
- 2/3 processed in meat grinder or food processor
- 1/3 finely diced
- 1 tbsp capers
- 1 tsp lemon juice
- 1 tbsp chopped herb, parsley, dill and chervil
- Salt, pepper, Worcestershire sauce and some juice from the capers, Tabasco to taste

Sauce:
- 1 cup sour cream or crème fraiche
- 1 tbsp chopped chive
- 2 tbsp diced, very ripe Roma tomato or vine ripe tomato
- Salt, pepper, lemon juice to taste

PREPARATION:
- For the burger mix all ingredients gently together, season to taste.
- Shape into hamburger size patties
- Grill to preferred temperature and serve on hamburger bun with traditional garnish
- For the sauce; mix all ingredients together, season to taste
- Prepare half hour before use to allow flavors to combine. Garnish with baby lettuce and balsamic dressing

FRUITS OF THE FOREST PIE

INGREDIENTS:

Crust
1 x 9-inch double crust pie

Filling:
* 5 1/2 cup mixture of ANY COMBINATION of summer fruits.

> Most popular in Alaska:
> 2 cups chopped rhubarb
> 1 cup blueberries
> 1 cup raspberries or strawberries
> 1/2 cup blackberries
> 1 cup sliced peaches or Granny Smith apples

* 3/4 cup sugar (more or less depending on how ripe the fruit is)
* 1/3 cup flour
* 2 tbsp. cornstarch
* 1/2 tsp. cinnamon
* 3 tbsp. lemon juice

PREPARATION:
* Preheat oven to 400°F. Prepare favorite two-pie-crust recipe. Place crust in large pie pan.
* Prepare fruit. Mix sugar, flour, cornstarch and cinnamon in large bowl. Gently stir in fruit to coat.
* Pour filling into prepared pie crust. Top with remaining crust and flute edges.
* Bake for about 40 - 45 minutes. Serve with vanilla ice cream or heavy cream.

ALASKAN SOURDOUGH PANCAKES

INGREDIENTS:

- 1 package starter or 1 cup "sourdough sponge"
- 2 cups flour
- 2 cups milk
- 2 eggs
- 1 tsp. soda
- 3 tbsp. sugar
- 1 tsp. salt
- 2 tsp. baking powder

PREPARATION:

- Put starter or sponge in large bowl. Add 2 cups flour and 2 cups milk. Mix well and cover.
- Leave in warm place overnight. Next morning take out 1 cup starter. Leave room temperature 12 hours.
- To remaining sponge add 2 eggs, 1 tsp soda, 2 tbsp sugar, 1 tsp salt, 2 tsp baking powder. Mix well. Cook on hot griddle.
- For smaller mixture take out 2 cups starter and use 1/2 the ingredients.
- Serve with your favorite syrup, preserves or fresh fruit

WHAT TO PACK

"The is no bad weather, only bad clothing!" German saying

Clothes
Alaska is not fancy. Anything goes. The operative word is layers! Dress for the weather, and since the weather changes all the time, prepare for anything. When the sun is out temperatures can soar into the 90's in the summer. But when the sky clouds up or the wind kicks in it can turn bitterly cold. Rain is almost a certainty so a light raincoat or poncho is a good idea. Take an insulated windbreaker, sweater and turtleneck if you plan on spending much time on the open decks of the ship or on smaller boats whale watching or fishing. If it heats up you can always peel it off. A hat, sunscreen and chap stick are mandatory. The sun stays higher in the sky longer on summer days this far north and the wind can be very drying. Good walking shoes and boots are preferable for the ship as well as in town.

Gear
A good light day pack is always handy. In it you can carry your binoculars, sunscreen, non-scented moisturizer, insect repellent, chap stick, hat, hand wipes, camera, extra batteries/film/memory stick, water/water bottle, change of socks, journal or note-pad, reference books or identification cards, GPS, and *The Cruiser Friendly Guide to Alaska's Inside Passage!*

Reminder
Don't forget your binoculars, water, insect repellant and sunscreen. Mosquitoes can be annoying in dense wooded areas – take along a DEET repellant if you plan on taking a long walk into their forest. Though it is a welcome sight, the sun's rays are more direct and damaging at this latitude. Remember sunburns can be caused by reflection off water and ice. The Caribbean's not the only place where sunburn can ruin your cruise!

CRUISING FOR THOSE WITH DISABILITIES

Onboard every effort is made to accommodate guests with any and all types of physical disabilities. Rooms with wider doors, no thresholds and specially-designed bathrooms are available for those with wheelchairs. Assistance is always available for help to and from public rooms as well as on and off the ship. However, even with the of best intentions passengers with disabilities may feel frustrated. Here's a reminder:

- Onboard as part of maritime safety, all outside doors have high thresholds. Ramps are usually provided, but you may run into an out-of-the-way spot where one is not provided.

- Buffets, a mainstay of cruise travel, are hard to navigate from a wheelchair and may require assistance.

- Lounges and areas from which passengers are most likely to view scenic sights, like glaciers, may be full with standing people. Crew and staff members are always willing to help make a place for you, so please don't miss the chance to experience what you came to Alaska to see. Ask for help. That's what we are here for!

Going ashore

Please note the following;
In Sitka all ships must anchor and use their ship's tenders to shuttle passengers ashore. Be advised that you will have to climb up and down the metal stairs to the tender landing and step onto and off the tender. Help is available. **Wheelchairs can be accommodated.** Please ask.

When getting on and off the tenders please accept the assistance of the uniformed crew members. Tenders move up and down. The crew is trained to know how and when it will rise and fall. Please follow their guidance.

- In Ketchikan and Juneau, tendering is also a possibility for your ship. Your travel agent should be able to tell you if you dock or tender. If you need help, please ask.

- In Skagway, though Skagway is a docked port, it has one of the highest tidal fluctuations in the world. Because of this the gangway can become very steep and may have to be moved or changed several times during your stay. If you need it, ask for help!

Once onshore, all state and local tourist facilities must abide by federal law regarding accessibility.

While onboard kindly remind your Guest Services manager if you have any allergies that require special attention.

GENERAL INFORMATION

AVERAGE SOUTHEAST TEMPERATURES

	Ketchikan	Juneau	Sitka	Skagway
January	34	25	33	22
February	39	28	37	27
March	39	33	41	33
April	43	40	45	41
May	49	47	47	49
June	54	53	52	55
July	58	56	54	58
August	58	55	57	57
September	54	49	53	50
October	46	42	45	42
November	39	33	38	31
December	35	27	35	26

AVERAGE PRECIPITATION

	Ketchikan	Juneau	Sitka	Skagway
January	14	4	8	2
February	12	4	6	2
March	12	3	6	1.4
April	12	3	5	1
May	9	3	4.4	1.4
June	7	3	3	1.3
July	8	4	4	1.2
August	11	5	6	2.3
September	14	6	11	3.6
October	22	8	14	4.6
November	18	5	9	2.5
December	16	5	9	3

AVERAGE ANNUAL SNOWFALL

Ketchikan	4.05	inches
Juneau	10.96	inches
Sitka	8.27	inches
Skagway	16.09	inches

SHIP STATISTICS

Ship's Name _____

Cruise Line _____

Year Built _____   Shipyard _____

Flag of Registry _____

Length _____   Beam _____

Height _____   Draft _____

Tonnage _____   Max. Speed _____

Number of decks _____   Number of pools _____

Number of bars _____   Number of restaurants _____

Maximum number of passengers _____

Number of passengers on this cruise _____

Number of Crew_____

People

Captain _____   Nationality _____

Cruise Director _____   Nationality _____

Stewardess _____   Nationality _____

Steward _____   Nationality _____

Favorite waiter/waitress _____

Favorite bartender _____

Favorite staff member _____

Places

Favorite port: _____

Favorite show: _____

Favorite memory: _____

_____

_____

_____

DAILY LOG AND CRUISE DIARY

DAY ONE

Date: _____

Port: _____

Arrival Time: _____

Departure Time:_____

Weather: _____

Comments: _____
_____
_____
_____
_____

DAY TWO

Date: _____

Port: _____

Arrival Time: _____

Departure Time: _____

Weather: _____

Comments: _____
_____
_____
_____

DAY THREE

Date: _____

Port: _____

Arrival Time: _____

Departure Time: _____

Weather: _____

Comments: _____
_____
_____
_____

DAY FOUR

Date: _____

Port: _____

Arrival Time: _____

Departure Time: _____

Weather: _____

Comments: _____
_____
_____
_____

DAY FIVE

Date: _____

Port: _____

Arrival Time: _____

Departure Time: _____

Weather: _____

Comments: _____
_____
_____
_____

DAY SIX

Date: _____

Port: _____

Arrival Time: _____

Departure Time: _____

Weather: _____

Comments: _____
_____
_____
_____

DAY SEVEN

Date: _____

Port: _____

Arrival Time: _____

Departure Time: _____

Weather: _____

Comments: _____
_____
_____
_____

NAUTICAL TERMS

Aft – Toward the stern of the ship

Ahead – Moving in a forward direction

Astern – In back of the ship, opposite of ahead

Aweigh – The position of the anchor when it is raised

Beam – Greatest width of the ship

Boat – A small craft carried aboard a ship

Bow – The forward part of the ship

Bridge – The location from which the Captain navigates the ship

Bulkhead – Walls or partitions separating compartments

Buoy – An anchored float marking a position in the water

Cable – Nautical measurement; 1/10th of a nautical mile = 608 feet

Cast off – To let go

Chart – Navigational map

Draft – The depth of water a ship draws

Ebb – Receding current

Fore – Toward the front of the ship

Fathom – Six feet

Flood – Incoming current

Galley – Kitchen on a ship

Gangway – Area of a ship where people board and disembark

Hull – Main body of a ship

Keel – Centerline of a ship, underwater spine

Knot – Measure of nautical speed; 6076 feet per hour

MV – Motor Vessel

Midship – Approximately in the middle of the ship, between bow and stern

Port – The left side of the ship as you face forward

SS – Steam Ship

SV – Sailing Vessel

Screw – Ship's propeller

Ship – A larger vessel thought to be used only for ocean travel

Slack – Loose

Sounding – A measurement of depth of water

Squall – Sudden rain storm

Starboard – The right side of the ship as you face forward

Stem – The most forward part of the bow

Stern – The back of the ship

Tender – Small boat carried by the ship used to ferry guests from ship to shore.

BIBLIOGRAPHY AND SUGGESTED READING

GENERAL:

Alaska Atlas & Gazetteer. DeLorme Mapping. Yarmouth: DeLorme Publishing, 1998.

Anderson, Bern. *The Life and Voyages of Captain George Vancouver.* Toronto: University of Toronto Press, 1966.

DeArmond, R.N. *Southeast Alaska Names on the Chart and How They Got There.* Juneau: Commercial Signs and Printing, 1995.

Fisher, Robin, ed. *From Maps to Metaphors: The Pacific World of Captain George Vancouver.* Vancouver: University of British Columbia Press, 1993.

Green, John. *Looking for Alaska.* New York: Dutton, 2005.

Hakkinen, Elizabeth. *A Personal Look at The Sheldon Museum & Cultural Center.* Juneau: Alaska State Museum, 1983.

Hayes, Derek. *Historical Atlas of the Pacific Northwest: Maps of Explanation and Discovery: British Columbia, Washington, Oregon, Alaska, Yukon.* Seattle: Sasquatch Books, 2002.

Klien, Maury. *The Life and Legend of E. H. Harriman.* Chapel Hill: University of North Carolina Press, 2000.

London, Jack. *Call of the Wild, White Fang, Sea Wolf, Klondike.* New York: Library of America, 1982

Michener, James. *Alaska.* New York: Fawcett Books, 1989.

Muir, John. *Travels in Alaska, 1915.* New York: Penguin Books, 1997.

Orth, Donald. *Dictionary of Alaska Place Names.* Anchorage: Glacier House Publishing, 1971.

Ryan, Alan. *The Reader's Companion to Alaska.* San Diego: Harcourt Brace, 1997.

Schorr, Alan Edward. *Alaska Place Names.* 4th ed. Juneau: The Denali Press, 1991.

Whitekeys, Mr. *The Alaska Almanac: Facts about Alaska.* Seattle: Alaska Northwest Books, 1999.

ALASKAN HISTORY:

Berton, Pierre. *Klondike: The Last Great Gold Rush 1896-1898.* Ontario: Anchor Canada, 2001.

Berton, Pierre. *The National Dream: The Great Railway 1871-1881.* Ontario: Anchor Canada, 2001.

Borneman, Walter. *Alaska: Saga of a Bold Land--From Russian Fur Traders to the Gold Rush, Extraordinary Railroads, World War II, the Oil Boom, and the Fight Over ANWR.* New York: HarperCollins, 2003.

Cohen, Stan. *The Forgotten War, Vol. I & II.* Missoula: Pictorial Histories Publishing, 2002.

Morgan, Lael. *Good Time Girls of the Alaskan Gold Rush.* Kenmore, Washington: Epicenter Press, 1999.

Murphy, Claire Rudolf, & Jane Haigh. *Gold Rush Women.* Seattle: Alaska Northwest Publications, 1997.

Ritter, Harry. *Alaska's History: The People, Land and Events of the North Country.* Seattle: Alaska Northwest Books, 1993.

Satterfield, Archie. *Chilkoot Pass: Then and Now.* Seattle: Alaska Northwest Books, 1973.

NATURAL HISTORY:

Akasofu, Syun-Ichi. *Aurora Borealis, The Amazing Northern Lights.* Fairbanks: Alaska Geographic, 1994.

Armstrong, Robert. *Guide to the Birds of Alaska.* Seattle: Alaska Northwest Books, 1995.

Bernard, Hannah, and Michele Morris. *The Oceanic Society Field Guide to the Humpback Whale.* Seattle: Sasquatch Books, 1993.

Connor, Cathy. *Roadside Geology of Alaska.* Missoula: Mountain Press Publishing, 1988.

Emanuel, Richard and Matz, George. *Exploring Alaska's Birds,* Anchorage: Alaska   Geographic Society, 2001.

Gordon, David and Chuck Flaherty. *The Oceanic Society Field Guide to the Orca.* Seattle: Sasquatch Books, 1990.

Kavanagh, James. *Alaska Birds.* Phoenix: Waterford Press, 2001.

Kavanagh, James. *Alaska Trees & Wildflowers.* Phoenix: Waterford Press, 2001.

Kavanagh, James, *Alaska Wildlife.* Phoenix: Waterford Press, 2001.

Smith, Dave. *Alaska's Mammals: A Guide to Selected Species.* Seattle: Alaska Northwest Publications, 1997.

Tekeila, Stan. *Birds of Alaska Field Guide.* Cambridge, MN: Adventures Publications, 2005.

NATIVE AMERICANS:

Christopher Cardozo, ed. *Sacred Legacy: Edward S. Curtis and the North American Indian.* New York: Simon and Schuster, 2000.

DeLaguna, Frederica. *Under Mount Saint Elias: The History and Culture of the Yakutat Tlingit."* 2nd ed. Ottawa, Canada: Federica de Laguna Northern Books, 2010.

Emmons, George Thornton. *The Tlingit History.* Anthropological Papers of the American Museum of Natural History. Seattle: University of Washington Press, 1991.

Hancock, David. *Tlingit: Their Art and Culture.* Blaine, Washington: Hancock House Publishing, 2003.

Holm, Bill. *Northwest Coast Indian Art: An Analysis of Form.* Seattle: University of Washington Press, 1965.

Jones, Veda Boyd. *Native Americans of The Northwest Coast.* San Diego: Greenhaven Press, 2000.

Kamenskii, Anotolii. *Tlingit Indians of Alaska.* Fairbanks: University of Alaska Press, 1985.

Langdon, Steven J. *The Native Peoples of Alaska.* Anchorage: Greatland Graphics, 1998.

Olson, Wallace. *Tlingit: An Introduction to Their Culture and History.* Auke Bay, Alaska: Heritage Research, 1997.

Stewart, Hilary. *Looking at Indian Art of the Northwest Coast.* Seattle: University of Washington Press, 1979.

Waterman, Thomas J. Tlingit Places Names for Extreme Southeast Alaska.

American Indian Quarterly 21 (1998) <questia.com/googleScholar.
qst?docId=76957926>.

ECONOMY AND ECOLOGY:

Banerjee, Subhanken. *Arctic National Wildlife Refuge: Seasons of the Life and
Land.* Foreward by Jimmy Carter. Seattle: Mountaineers Books, 2003.

Matz, George. *"Money Trees: Alaska's Timber Industry." Alaska Business
Monthly* v11 (1995): 48-51.

Ott, Riki. *Not One Drop: Betrayal and Courage in the Wake of the Exxon
Valdez Oil Spill.* White River Junction, Vermont: Chelsea Green Publishing,
2008.

Sabella, John, director. *Fishing for the Future: The Southeast Alaskan Salmon
Industry.* VHS Video. Port Townsend, Washington: John Sabella and Associates,
Inc, 1998.

GOLD MINING:

Janes, Wilete. *In the Miners' Footsteps: An Historic Overview and Guide to
the Mining Trails in the Juneau-Douglas Area,* 5th ed. Gastineau Channel
Historical Society. Juneau: Taku Graphics, 2004.

Redman, Earl. *History of the Mines and Miners in the Juneau Gold Belt: a
Collection of Stories Telling about the Mines, the Miners, their Golden
Dreams and How They Tried to Achieve Them.* Washington, D. C.: Bureau of
Mines, 1987.

Rennick, Penny. *Juneau: Yesterday and Today.* Anchorage, Alaska: Alaska
Geographic Society, 2003.

Stone, David and Brenda. *Hard Rock Gold : the Story of the Great Mines that
Were the Heartbeat of Juneau.* Juneau, Alaska: Juneau Centennial Committee,
1980, 1982.

RESOURCES:

Alaska Department of Fish and Game. *Wildlife News,* Division of Wildlife
Conservation. Article archive site: < www.wc.adfg.state.ak.us/index.
cfm?adfg=wildlife_news.archive>.

Alaska State Department of Natural Resources, Office of History and Archaeology,
Alaska Geographic Names Program <dnr.alaska.gov/parks/oha/histcomm/
aknames.htm>.

Cornwall, David, Government Publications Librarian, Alaska State Library, Juneau.

Truffer, Martin, PhD, University of Alaska, Fairbanks, Department of Geology/ Glacial Studies.

United States Government Survey. USGS Geographic Names Information System. 1 May 2009 <geonames.usgs.gov>.

Alaska Community Database: CIS (Communication Information Summaries). Valdez Chamber of Commerce, <www.commerce.state.ak.us/dca/commdb/CIS. cfm>.

PHOTO CREDITS

Copyrighted photos used with permission of owner:

Mike Roemhild -	X, 5, 58, 105, 118, 170, 175, 233-237
David Edwards	XVI, 70-71
P. Fichet-Delavault -	14, 40, 132, 145, 148
Mike Baird -	19,
Terry Breen -	38, 43, 53, 54, 83, 97, 123-125
Elda Pauluzzi -	42,
Edward Curtis -	48, 49, 50, 56
Jeremy Keith -	51
Larry Bourne -	110
Andrei from NY -	245
Eric McAtee -	82
Sylvain Laferrière -	1

Photos used under the Creative Commons license:

Carl Chapman-	31
Len Turner-	32
Grace Kelly-	25
Derek Ramsey-	68
JuWiki2-	101
Armadilo60 (flickr)-	137
Víctor J. Tornet-	178

creativecommons.org/licenses/by/3.0/

*All other photos used under the definition of "Free Cultural Works" as works or expressions which can be freely studied, applied, copied and/or modified, by anyone, for any purpose.

SPECIAL THANKS

To the Tlingit artists, designer George Benson and carver Herman Kitka of the Te Kot Keh Yago (Everybody's Canoe) in Sitka Alaska. (Page 54)

To Tlingit artist Nathan Jackson for his carving of the mural in the Cape Fox Hotel in Ketchikan, Alaska. (Page 125)

INDEX

BIOGRAPHY

Terry Breen

A cultural anthropologist by training, for the past twenty years Terry has worked on the most prestigious cruise ships in the world. She has used her academic experience to transition to the world of travel where in-depth knowledge of people and places is essential. She pioneered the position of ship's regional expert, the onboard resource person for all things pertaining to the destination. She is author of The Cruiser Friendly Onboard Guide series including *The Cruiser Friendly Onboard Guide to Alaska's Inside Passage, The Cruiser Friendly Onboard Guide to The Panama Canal* and *The Cruiser Friendly Onboard Guide to Exploring the Antarctic Peninsula*. She has lived and traveled throughout Latin America and was employed by several international airlines and regional tourism boards. In 1990, she traded her wings for waves when she first began working onboard cruise ships in South America. As of 2011, she has sailed around Cape Horn 44 times and through the Panama Canal 78 times!

Mary Sterner Lawson

A native of Ohio who holds a Ph.D. in English from Bowling Green State University and a professor of English at Albany State University from 1973-2004, she retired to Tallahassee in 2004. An exhibiting artist in Georgia and Florida since the mid-eighties, Lawson primarily works in pen and ink and watercolor. Months spent in Finland and the Netherlands, two Fulbright-Hays month-long programs to China and Brazil, and extensive travels outside the United States have provided subject matter for scores of ink drawings and paintings. She came back from her first visit to China with over 200 drawings. During her 32 years of university life, hours and hours of lengthy academic meetings honed her portrait sketching skills. In fact, the president of the university from which she retired borrowed her sketches of faculty and staff members and had them scanned into the university archives. A 1996 painting by Lawson, *June Bug's Grocery*, led to a massive oral history project focusing on a South Albany African American community that was devastated by a catastrophic flood in 1994. Her book, *June Bug's Grocery and the Cornfield Jook: A South Albany Oral History,* was published by Arcadia Publishing Company in 2003. Currently Lawson writes and paints at her home studio in Tallahassee, Florida.